CONTENTS

	Editor's Note	7
1	The Rock	9
2	Shirts, Tattie-Hoking and Salt Herring	16
3	Room to Rhyme	25
4	Sarida	37
5	'Kent-Men', the Flu and Hot Sermons	47
6	Black and Tans	53
7	Auxies and Ballads	62
8	Erin's Pride – and a New Police Force	71
9	The 'Rabbles'	79
10	Iskaheen	90
11	Hired Again	96
12	Kilrea Fair and a Winter at Home	106
13	On the Rocks	114
14	Triple Alliance	123
15	The Heysham Boat and Tom Mix	130
16	The Barn	141
17	Golf and Fit-ba'	155
18	Making Hay . . .	162
19	Tunnel Tiger	171
20	The Boo-geers of Traws	179
21	Guardsman	190
22	Iris	203
23	Living on Love	212
24	Landscape Gardener, Film Extra or Linesman?	219

25 On the Beach   227
26 All Aboard *The Medway Queen*   237
27 '...No More Soldiering for Me!'   249

EDITOR'S NOTE

That Was the Way of It was quarried from a much larger typescript of nearly 170,000 words written towards the end of the 1980s. In it my Uncle Paddy told his own story, describing a career that took him from his birthplace in the Rock, a rural district north-east of Buncrana in Inishowen, to, among other places, the beach at Dunkirk in June 1940. There, sheltering among the dunes and hoping for a miraculous rescue, he wondered many times if his career might have an abrupt finish.

My selection of text leans naturally towards his account of his childhood and youth in Ireland, and the chapters which deal with these early days amount to approximately two-thirds of the book. I was tempted to stop there, since this material makes a fascinating book in its own right. Yet Paddy's account of highlights of his adult life, especially his war experiences, is so graphic and entertaining that it seemed a pity not to include something of them.

I have thought it appropriate to interpose a little editorial explanation to introduce these later chapters and give a brief résumé of the autobiographical details that are not included in the remaining text. I must here express my indebtedness to a number of people who played their parts in the creation of this book: Rose Doherty (née Grant), who was perhaps Paddy's favourite niece and who shares her uncle's memory and storytelling ability; Andy McLaughlin and his wife Sarah, without whose timely interest and interventions the original manuscript might never have been copied and brought to Ireland; and finally Denis Bradley, whose Big Hill father was a contemporary of the author.

1
—

THE ROCK

A peninsula is a small portion of land that is almost surrounded by water and juts out into the sea. This was how my schoolmistress always described it during geography lessons. Perhaps she was reminding the class of its whereabouts at the time, because Inishowen in north-east Donegal well fits such a description. Bounded on the east by Lough Foyle and on the west by Lough Swilly, Inishowen juts into the North Atlantic at Malin Head. The two approach roads are Derry–Moville on the Foyle side and Derry–Buncrana on the Swilly side. The latter I know best; at home we always called it 'Burncrina'.

Buncrana is a well-known holiday resort and the approach road runs alongside the famous Lisfannon golf links. Three miles north of Buncrana there is a crossroads. If you take the left fork over Dunian bridge and the next turning right, in no time you will be in a place called 'the Rock', in the townland of Fofenagh. In my childhood days you couldn't go any further: there was no through-road. In those times the Rock was a small community of six families, some thirty or more souls in all. Each family owned a narrow strip of land of the poorest quality known as 'the Moss', which ran down to the main road. Behind each house, and sheltered by cairns and stone ditches, were additional bits of land where famous potatoes called Irish Whites always flourished. Since potatoes boiled in their jackets, peeled and dipped in salt and pepper constituted the main meal every day, Irish Whites were crucial to the economy of the Rock.

The three hills overlooking the Rock are Malia, Cnoc Brac and Tructrasna. These were common grazing land and, although mainly bracken and heather, gave food and shelter to a few sheep and one or two cows of a hardy breed called galloways. The hills also provided good shelter for the small houses nestling below. Tructrasna is a bit out of line with the other two, as if a great earth-moving machine had gouged a slice from between Malia and Crow Brac and dumped its load well forward. The gap that was left is called 'Paul Dugh' and acts as a funnel for the fierce winds blowing from the north-west. Even in calm weather there is always a breeze in Paul Dugh. But its nooks and crannies gave great shelter to those engaged in 'wee-still' making (poteen). No excise or policeman could reach Paul Dugh unobserved in daylight, and none were brave enough to attempt it once darkness fell.

As a wee boy I spent many a blissful hour on Crow Brac, where there are traces of an old slate quarry. Embedded in the slates were little nuggets of quartz. I would hammer away at the slates until the nuggets were freed, and carry them around in my pocket, pretending they were gold. Later, Crow Brac was included in a geological survey. Two very studious-looking gentlemen with goatee beards arrived and spent a whole day tapping the slates with little hammers.

When evening came, they departed, taking with them a little canvas bag full of 'fool's gold'. Their visit soon gave rise to rumours that a precious metal had been found and that the Rock was on the brink of becoming a new El Dorado. However, when their survey report was published a year or two later, Crow Brac got only a brief mention. It seemed that the nugget phenomenon had occurred somewhere in Wales also, leading the experts to believe that it had something to do with the movement of the land mass during the Ice Age. So the Rock managed to escape the march of progress and kept its tranquillity. I hope it continues to do so forever.

The only thing that seemed odd about my family name was its scarcity. I can only remember hearing of three other families named 'Devlin'. They lived in Moville, Clonmany and Fahan respectively. Irish genealogical records suffered badly in penal times. To remove any traces of their origin, the names of people and places were given more British-sounding titles. But the worst blow of all fell in 1922. The national archives, which were housed in the Dublin Four Courts, were destroyed. New records had to be compiled from the salvage, and no doubt there are many gaps unfilled. From what information there is available, the name 'Devlin' first occurred in hyphenated form in 1256. Its owner was one Adam De Divelyn. It occurred again in 1380, with a William Develyn. The Irish versions were Ó Dobhailín or Ó Doibhilín. Holders of these names had an inheritance of some kind in County Tyrone but they were dispossessed and afterwards turned to the professions of law, politics and journalism, so the story goes. But no such fame spread to my family, the 'Divilins' of the Rock, as we were called. Maybe it was because we were surrounded on all sides, and well outnumbered, by Dohertys and Grants, that I was called in to strengthen the ranks. For, according to a copy of my birth certificate, I joined the little community of the Rock on 16 March 1909. This document also records another notable entry. In the space for father's signature it reads 'His Mark', followed by an 'X'. But what a gentle and kind man he was, with many attributes more than compensating for his inability to write.

I was the youngest of a family of eight – three boys and five girls – and therefore the youngest son. The position of a third son, or even a second, was very precarious in those days. The smallholding was usually bequeathed to the eldest son. Since there was no local employment, the others were destined to head for the boat, or 'buy the steam', as we used to say, as soon as they were old enough to do so. It seems, however, that I wasn't prepared to wait that long, for I ran away from home when I was about two years old. It appears that I was going quite well until one of my sisters grabbed me just as I was about to venture on to the main road. The only excuse I had to offer for my runaway behaviour was that I knew my granny lived somewhere nearby, in a place called Sarida. I remembered from a previous visit that she kept some lovely sweets called brandy balls. Ever since time began, grannies have been accused of spoiling their grandchildren. But in the heart and mind of a child, granny, with her little bag of sweets, was the only one who could manage to sprinkle a little stardust. The last I recall of that grand old lady was the day she was laid to rest. It was a very hot day in July, and in the afternoon a violent thunderstorm, complete with a 'water-spout', broke. Heavy floods devastated crops, and the haycocks near the River Crana were swept away.

But now, alas and all too soon, my carefree days were drawing to an end: it was time to join in the age-old quest for the truth and commence school. So one fine morning my dear mother handed me over to the tender mercies of Master Joseph Kearney and his able assistant Miss Curran at Kinnego National School. Master Kearney was an esteemed figure, a lifelong bachelor and a strict disciplinarian. But he was fair, rarely administering the cane to one hand only, mostly to both, so that both aching hands could sympathize with each other. Another technique for which he was famous was known as 'dusting the jacket': he raised many a cloud of dust by a resounding whack across the shoulders with his cane. He had his own philosophy on how wee boys should be dealt with, as one irate parent found out when he lodged a complaint about the harsh treatment meted out to his son. Master Kearney's answer was that wee boys should always be beaten, every time you met them – because if they weren't coming from doing mischief, they were on their way to do some.

For all that, he was a great teacher, always taking great pains to enlighten the older scholars, while Miss Curran laboured valiantly with us juniors. I suppose it was inevitable that one day she and I would reach a misunderstanding; the blow fell during a catechism lesson. We were repeating the line from the 'Hail Holy Queen': 'To thee we send up our sighs.' 'Patrick,' says she, 'come out in front of the class and repeat that last line again.' I did so at once. But when a wave of sniggering and giggling went round the class, I realised I had made an almost blasphemous statement: 'To thee we send up our sides.' It took a long time to live that one down, but I made up for it by being a great one for the geography. While the others were pondering aimlessly, trying to find places on the map, Miss Curran would say, 'Patrick, show them.' I took a great delight in doing so. Miss Curran was always immaculately dressed and, with just enough perfume to be noticed, she always smelled pretty. Both teachers cycled daily, in all weathers, from Buncrana to Kinnego and home again. I can't recall either of them ever missing a single day.

The Kinnego Flute Band provided the main attraction for us boys in those days. Its instruments were housed near the school in an empty house called 'Jane the Cobbler's'; the house was also used as a practice room. The band at odd times even had the services of an instructor. Mr Shields was his name but we always called him 'Ould Shales'. He was an ex-army drum major and a man who had seen better times. I believe his remuneration was by way of a liberal supply of the 'hard stuff' instead of cash. In his absence, the band would practise in small groups. I can remember my eldest brother James, Mick's Willie and his brother Mick doing flute practice in our house while Pat's Daniel drummed on an upturned bucket and my father beat time on the side of the settle-bed with a pair of tongs. Of them all, Mick's Willie was the most conscientious student, and on the long summer evenings he would sit outside and practise the musical scales. But soon all the dogs in the Rock would join him in a kind of vocal refrain. It was a great howl-on altogether. When the band was on parade, its central figure was the bass drummer 'Big Mickey' from Kinnego. The musical technique of drumming wasn't one of Mickey's strong points: he believed the harder the drums was beaten, the better the result. So, with jacket off and sleeves rolled up, Mickey would give the drum a powerful hammering.

St Patrick's Day was the occasion of the big parade. It was traditional on such occasions for the band to have a full escort of pikemen. This honour went to the tallest men in the neighbourhood: men like Pat Ellemy, Matthew Lynch, Charlie's Johnnie, Mick Hegarty and Paddy Bradley, to name but a few. They all shouldered long-handled pikes with gleaming gold-painted tips and wore colourful sashes of green and gold. Every man had a bunch of shamrock in his cap and an 'Erin Go Bragh' badge in his lapel. So, with drums beating and flags flying, the band would set off in grand array for Mass at Cockhill. Among them was a fine young flute player, Joe's Owen, who later joined the Civic Guards and became a leading instrumentalist in the Dublin Police Band. So maybe Ould Shales's efforts weren't wasted after all.

Sadly, in the end the Kinnego Flute Band fell victim to emigration, the scourge of our nation, when many of its youthful members had to set sail for America. They left behind them many lonely lanes, particularly in evenings. My eldest brother James was amongst them; he had to hand in his flute but he left me his old tin whistle, which I treasured for many a day. Many years later I was to have the unique experience of marching through the streets of London, led by famous bands of the Brigade of Guards. I sometimes thought that, for all their style and splendour, perhaps Big Mickey knew a trick or two about drumming which the Guards hadn't thought about. Anyway, it was a pleasant thought at the time.

2

—

Shirts, Tattie-Hoking and Salt Herring

One effect of the First World War was to give a slight
boost to the economy of the Rock. Extra work of a kind
was created for the womenfolk. Derry, the main base for
the shirt-making industry, was no longer able to cope with
the demands of army contracts. Subsidiary factories were
set up in nearby towns, so Buncrana became a busy centre
for shirt-making. The material, already cut to pattern,
came to the centre in large bales. From there, it had to
be collected by horse and cart; the finished product was
returned in the same manner. The work was then in-
spected by the overseers, members of a family named
Malseed; heavy deductions from pay were imposed for
work not up to standard. So it was that, from early
morning until late at night, nearly every house in the
neighbourhood hummed with the sound of sewing machines. I can remember my dear mother and elder sisters
machining away and sewing on buttons, toiling from early
morning until bedtime trying to get their quota done on
time. In return they received the princely sum of two
shillings per dozen, or tuppence per shirt. There was also

a great demand for wool, and those who had access to big grazing areas and could afford to increase their stock did so profitably. A deposit of low-grade iron ore was discovered in the neighbourhood; it was dug up and carted to Ballymagan station and despatched to the furnaces of war somewhere.

In those days, we in the Rock were badly handicapped by the lack of news. Important events were unfolding worldwide but by the time an old copy of the *Journal* reached us, the news had gone stale. We relied heavily on Charley Blue the postman to keep us abreast of current affairs; although Charley's information was well laced with rumour and speculation, it was better than no news at all. When a week-old copy of the *Journal* did reach us, I can remember nearly all the men in the Rock gathering in our house on a Sunday afternoon to hear it being read. Maybe this arrangement saved waiting for the paper to be passed from house to house. I suspect, however, that it was because not all the men could read. Hughdie's Willie was the exception, though: he was not only an avid reader but a stickler for detail as well. But first Willie had to get his specs in focus; there were no earpieces, so he improvised with a piece of string wound round each ear. When the specs were correctly balanced, somewhere near the end of his nose, Willie would begin. He would lead off with the name of the paper and the date of publication, which was generally sometime a week previous. Then on to the war reports, which dominated the headlines at the time. One particular war despatch seemed to come from the same place at the same time every week, and was always headed Amsterdam, Sunday, 2 pm.

Although it seemed to be a safe distance from the front line, Willie never missed it and always presented it as 'Amsterdam Sunday 2 pim.'

The main political figure hogging the headlines at the time was Lloyd George, and the mere mention of his name was enough to put Willie into a tantrum. On one occasion, when a banner headline read 'Lloyd George Calls for Ten Thousand More Volunteers', Willie nearly broke a blood vessel. 'Bad luck to that ould Welsh druid,' Willie said. 'He'll get us all kill't yet.'

I don't know if the war economy brought much relief to the people of the Rock; there never seemed to be much cash about. We still relied on the old barter system: eggs and home-made butter were exchanged for small quantities of tea, sugar and flour. Debts would accrue to the local shopkeepers, to be paid off when an animal was sold or cash became available from some other source. Extra cash had to be earned abroad, usually at the Scotch harvests. Every year the head of the household, after he had done the spring planting and cut enough turf for the coming winter, would head for Scotland. Some would spend a week or two in England first: the hay harvest in Lancashire was usually earlier than elsewhere. Renfrew and Stirlingshire in Scotland were the areas where the men went regularly every year for the hay harvest. Later in the season they would move south to Berwickshire for the corn harvest and spud-lifting, or 'tattie-hoking', as it was called, before returning home in late autumn. In the men's absence, the womenfolk had to look after things at home as best they could.

Many a time I heard my father talk about his experiences as a harvester. He would recall the times when, as a lad, he accompanied my grandfather to the Scotch harvests, in the days when they even had to provide their own reap-hooks. I don't know what their rates of pay were, but no doubt they were minimal; the food and living conditions were very bad also. The practice was to work in small gangs; probably as many as six harvesters would be employed on one farm. They slept rough in barns and received one meal a day: breakfast. This was a large basin of porridge ('brochan', we called it at home), shared out among the gang. For the rest of their meals, they were allowed as many potatoes as they wanted, providing they cooked them themselves. Apart from the bad conditions on the farms, the harvesters had another problem to contend with: the anti-Irish attitude of the Scots. This amounted almost to hatred: the harvesters were usually referred to as 'Irish tramps'. The biggest culprit for this kind of abuse was the farm foreman, a character known as the 'hine'. He made life as difficult as possible for them on every occasion. Yet, in spite of all the difficulties, there was the odd occasion for a good laugh, like the morning the porridge arrived without any milk being added.

The harvesters were totally unaware that, unbeknown to her employer, a wee servant-girl had been adding milk to the porridge, purely out of sympathy for the harvesters. A man called Wee Pat was delegated to take the porridge back, since everyone believed a genuine oversight had occurred about the milk. Pat knocked on the back door, not knowing it was the wee girl's day off. As he waited, and the wonderful aroma of eggs and bacon being prepared for the family breakfast drifted towards him, his gastric juices became very lively. Presently the mistress herself came to the door and Pat stated his business about the missing milk. 'What milk?' the lady asked. 'How long have you been getting milk?' she wanted to know. By now Pat was trying hard to keep a civil tongue in his head, but his patience was diminishing fast and indeed vanished altogether when the lady said: 'Milk for Irish tramps indeed. Take it away and sup it and consider yourselves lucky to get porridge.' Pat couldn't hold out any longer and, before the lady had time to shut the door, he emptied the basin of porridge on her head. 'Aw, sup it yersel', ye cat-faced ould hoor ye,' he shouted, as he ran like hell back to the barn. In a very agitated state, Pat tried to explain to the others what had happened. He felt sure they would all get the sack when the good lady told her husband. Later on, the farmer came to the barn with another basin of porridge, well laced with milk. He wanted to know which brave man had had the audacity to empty a basin of porridge on the mistress's 'heed'. Pat owned up manfully and apologised profusely: he said he couldn't explain his behaviour, that something had come over him and that he was very sorry. 'I shouldnae fret yersel',' the farmer told him. For there was many a time in the past thirty years when he'd wanted to do something like that himself, he said, but somehow he'd never got round to it.

The harvesters liked to ensure that there was always someone in the gang who could count a few figures. They didn't trust the 'hines' when it came to squaring up the wages at the end of the harvest. My father remembered one farm where, directly the harvest was finished, the farmer and his wife went off on holiday, leaving the hine to square up the harvesters. This particular character went about the job as if it was an army pay parade. He had a table out in the yard and the gang had to line up in alphabetical order. When the pay packets were checked, it was found that each one was a half-crown short – a lot of money in those days. They challenged the hine on the spot, but he told them to get the hell off the farm before he sent for the 'polis'. The harvesters knew he was bluffing because the nearest 'polis' were miles away. Then one of the gang took charge of the proceedings. He ordered one man to shut the yard gate and another to fetch the small can of paraffin. Then he said to the hine: 'Ye can pay us the half-crown ye owe us, or we'll burn yer ould corn-stecks to the ground, one at a time!' This was too much for the hine. He threw the remaining half-crowns at the men, telling them he would make sure they never got a job on the farm again. But the harvesters weren't the least concerned: they were going home.

Some seasons, the harvest work finished a week or two earlier than usual. On his way home my father would stop off at Glasgow or Greenock and try to boost his earnings by casual labour on the docks. Working conditions on the farms may have been bad but on the docks they were atrocious. Most casual labour was employed on unloading iron ore which came from Spain. The ore was loaded into creels and carried on the men's backs up ladders from the ship's hold and dumped on the dockside. The gangs employed on this labour were known as the ore-carriers and were paid threepence a ton. The coaling of ocean-going ships was done by the same method, when fourpence a ton could be earned. The stevedores were the main employers of casual labour on the docks, and they were hard taskmasters. Frequently when the gang boss noticed the men were getting tired, he would sack them and hire a fresh gang. Because of poor pay and bad working conditions, disputes, stoppages and strikes were an almost daily occurrence. My father would sometimes spend a whole day on the docks and earn only ninepence. There was a small union on the docks trying to create order out of chaos; it was known as the National Union of Dock Labourers, which I believe was the forerunner of the now-powerful Transport and General Workers Union. The organiser responsible for the docks was little heard of at that time. Later, however, his name was writ large and emblazoned across the pages of trade union history, particularly in Ireland. His name was Jim Larkin.

As the war continued, times in the Rock grew harder and food was scarce and very dear. When our lifeline, the Irish Whites, ran out at the end of the season, we had to fall back on the old substitute, Indian brochan. Indian meal was a by-product of maize which came from America during famine times. Basically it was an animal food and reasonably cheap, and since we in the Rock could afford only the cheapest, Indian brochan became part of our natural heritage. For all that, there were certain times in the year when a wee boy, providing he was industrious, could augment the family larder considerably. Buncrana in those days was a busy fishing port, and herring trawlers from Scotland would arrive in the spring and autumn to unload their catches. Early in the morning while it was still dark, I would set off for Buncrana with a wee bag under my oxter. I would make my way to the pier and join lots of other wee boys who were lying in wait for the herring carts to pass on their way to the curing area. As the loaded carts left the pier there was a little brae, which the horses had to negotiate at the trot. Consequently the slippery herrings would slide over the tailboard onto the road. Then there would be a mad scramble, with much elbowing and pushing, to gather the herrings off the road before the next cart came along.

Sometimes the cart-owners, if there was no one around, would dive their hands into the load and scoop off a few extra herrings for us. By the time the trawlers were unloaded, I would have as many herrings as I could carry over the three miles back to the Rock. My contributions would be cleaned and salted down in a tub for use later. A good salt herring roasted on the turf fire took a bit of beating for tea on a cold winter's evening. Maybe that was why both our teachers turned a blind eye to the absence of wee boys from school during the herring season.

With the trawlers came the herring-gutters, and what a hardy, no-nonsense breed of women they were. Many of the younger ones would attend our local dances, or 'big nights', as they were called. They were all good dancers and there were some fine singers among them too; most of them spoke Gaelic and in this respect had the edge on us locals. They tended to look upon us as unfortunate victims of the subculture. But they had no objection to being escorted to and from dances by our local young men, though I believe this was strictly on a 'goodnight' and 'thank you' basis. No 'hanky-panky' was permitted. I did hear tell of some local lads who had the mistaken impression that these girls might be more adventurous in some respects, compared with the local girls. But the lads changed their minds after getting their comeuppance at the hands of some good-looking herring-gutter.

So bad was our lack of information about what was happening in the world around us that one of the most momentous events in Irish history had taken place while we in the Rock, except for the odd garbled account by Charley Blue, were totally unaware of its significance. It was the Easter Rising in Dublin in 1916. By the time we did get a full account from an out-of-date copy of the *Journal*, fifteen of Ireland's finest men were preparing to face the firing squad. As a consequence, although we might not have heard of some of them before, their names were now indelibly marked in the hearts and minds of both young and old alike throughout the land: names like Connolly, Clarke, MacDonagh, Pearse, Plunkett, MacBride and others. Although no one knew what was to follow, there was a feeling in the air that somehow things would never be the same again.

3

ROOM TO RHYME

It is often said that old customs, like old habits, die hard. I
believe, however, that some old customs lived longer in
Inishowen than anywhere else. Steeped in folklore and
mythology, the origin of some customs was always obscure.
I witnessed some and participated in others but never found
out how they originated. One that comes readily to mind is
the ceremony of the rush cross. It would be after dark on
an evening in late autumn. My father would knock on the
door and make an announcement in Gaelic. My mother, also
speaking in Gaelic, would bid him enter. He would stand in
the centre of the kitchen with two small bunches of rushes,
bound together in the shape of a cross. He would address
my mother again, and when she replied he would proceed
to nail the cross to one of the fir beams in the roof. Some
people believed the rush cross was a form of thanksgiving
for the safe gathering in of the crops. Others believed that
it was an act of homage to a very saintly person who
travelled through Inishowen centuries before, bringing relief
to the sick and dying. She was a Mother Teresa of her time
and was known as Saint Bríd, the Mary of the Gael.

Another custom, in which I was an enthusiastic participant, was cart stealing. This ritual took place once a year; maybe, for those whose carts were stolen, once a year was enough. Hallow Eve was the night for cart stealing but no harm was intended and there was no rancour afterwards. The cart stealers would spend the night playing cards until well past bedtime. The victims had to be selected with great care. Would the owner be able to run fast enough to catch up with us? Did he have a dog that would bark on our approach and give the game away? Of course, it would be a simple matter just to go to someone's premises, grab a cart and run off with it. But that wouldn't be cart stealing according to the rules. To do the job properly meant that the owner didn't know his cart was missing until he woke up next morning. Stealth, then, was the secret of success but at least half a dozen strong young men were required also. The fastest runner in the gang would creep forward in stockinged feet and position himself near the door, ready to grab the latch should anyone try to get out. The rest of the gang would then creep forward, lift the cart clear of the ground and remove the wheels. The wheels would be carried or trundled away noiselessly to the grass verge; then the cart would be carried until all was well clear of the premises. As soon as the cart was reassembled, off we would go like the hammers of hell.

At least four stealings were needed to make the night a success. The carts would be left in a field near the crossroads. Next day being a holy day, everyone, including the owners of the carts, would have to pass the crossroads on their way to Mass. In the afternoon the owners would bring their horses to retrieve their property, only to find themselves confronted by another problem. The cartwheels had all been swapped round, so most of the afternoon had to be spent sorting out which wheels belonged to which cart. But none of us cart stealers was around to hear their comments. I doubt if pranks and capers of that kind would be treated so lightly today. Most likely we would all finish up in jail. But who the hell would want to steal an old tractor, anyway?

The next old custom in which I was fortunate enough to play a lively part was Christmas rhyming. The origins of rhyming have never been fully explained. Many experts in Irish folklore have given their opinions, but the characters portrayed have proved difficult to elucidate. Rhyming was a mixture of historical, religious and mythological representations, the main feature being disguise. Almost every county had its own particular version, while in the south of Ireland and in some parts of Britain it was known as 'mumming'. At home, the rhyming season commenced as soon as the nights were dark enough – in late October – and lasted until a week or so before Christmas. Our troupe consisted of six men and a wee boy: me! Why I was chosen I don't know; perhaps I was the only wee boy handy at the time. I was given a rhyme scribbled on a piece of paper and told to learn it off by heart. The men dressed in a very symbolic manner indeed; disguise seemed to be the main aim of their outfits. They wore white shirts over their ordinary clothes, fastened at the waist by a belt. Belts with buckles of an ornate design were much sought after by rhymers. Sunday boots and leggings were worn and kept highly polished. Each man carried a walking stick, not so much to be used as a walking aid as to signal his entrance by two raps on the door. The most spectacular item of a rhymer's outfit was the headdress. Made out of cardboard, very tall, and square to the front, a small mirror or large brooch, which would reflect light, was mounted in the centre. In the dimly lit houses, the rhymer's disguise had a very profound effect indeed.

The only odd man out as regards dress was me. This was because my role as 'Divil Doubt' called only for my blackened face. Shoe-polish was ideal for the purpose but it was expensive, so I had to make do with soot from the chimney. It was considered unlucky to refuse admission to rhymers, so in that respect we had the wind at our backs most of the way. Floors would be cleared and tables and chairs pushed back to give us room. Indeed, room was what the first rhymer to enter a house called for. With two raps on the door, he would make his entrance with:

Room! Room! My gallant boys,
Give me room to rhyme!
I've come to show you some activity
About the Christmas time.
Actors young or actors aged,
The likes of me you'll never see
On any stage.
If you don't believe what I say.
I'll call in [the next character]
And he'll soon clear the way!

Most of the characters portrayed were either patriots or tyrants of Irish history. There was a rhyme dedicated to one personality who, whatever else he might have been, certainly wasn't one of Ireland's benefactors, Oliver Cromwell:

> *Here comes I, Oliver Cromwell,*
> *With my long copper nose.*
> *I've conquered many nations*
> *And Germany, I suppose.*

When all the rhymers had entered and said their piece, it was my turn. My cue was when the last rhymer announced: 'I'll call in wee Divil Doubt and he'll soon clear the way.' This was my moment of truth. So, with my old cap well down over my eyes, and trying hard to disguise the immaturity of my voice, I chanted:

> *Here comes I, Divil Doubt,*
> *The best wee divil*
> *That ever went out.*
> *Money I want and money I crave.*
> *If I don't get money.*
> *I'll sweep ye all away to yer grave.*

Having said my piece, I was expected to make a lot of noise, leap around the floor and frighten the womenfolk. Usually I was the one most frightened, especially as I tried to get close enough for the soot to rub off my face and onto theirs. But there was the odd pleasant surprise; according to some of the women, I was a 'right wee divil'. Now it was time for the business side of rhyming to be enacted. One of the rhymers would produce a small rattlebox: a tobacco tin with a pebble inside. He would shake the box to the following rhyme:

Here's a wee box
That speaks without a tongue.
One or two shillings
Will do it no wrong.
If you haven't got a shilling
Sixpence will do.
If you haven't got sixpence
Then God bless you.

At this point the head of household would make his, or her, donation. A shilling was about average, but there were many sixpences and, no matter how hard the times, we were never refused. When the money had been collected, the whole troupe sang:

Oh, we didn't come to your door
To beg nor to borrow,
But we came to your door
To drive away all sorrow.
With your pockets full of money
And your barrels full of beer
We wish you a merry Christmas
And a happy New Year.
So it's all for the drink.
That we sing, boys, sing!

Then, after a formidable rendering of some local ballad, we would make our exit in reverse order, the first man in being the last to leave. His departing message was always: 'God bless this house.'

The parish was more or less our stage. We covered a

wide area over rough roads in all weathers but we were young. Starting as soon as it was dark in the evening, we worked until ten o'clock. It was considered unmannerly to disturb people after that time. But I do remember one occasion when our ten o'clock rule had to be waived by request. On our way home we had to pass a house which was so well lit-up it was obvious a wedding was in progress. We intended to mind our own business and go on home, until two gentlemen stopped us, one being the best man. They insisted that we gave a performance just for good luck's sake for the newly-weds. In we went and gave a star performance. The men knew they were on to a good thing, because the very strict no-drinking rule could now be abandoned for the rest of the night. For me there was food galore and, being famished, I made the best of it. Next day I found it difficult trying to explain why I didn't get home until three in the morning.

There was another occasion when our ten o'clock rule wasn't appreciated by everyone. We had decided to give this particular house a miss. The owner, a very old lady, lived alone; we knew she went to bed early, and it would be a shame to disturb her. Next day, however, one of the rhymers received a little note and a sixpence sent by the old lady. She told us we were the worst set of rhymers ever to roam the countryside in her time. Didn't she wait up till all hours for us last night and we never came near nor by? We could have her sixpence but as far as she was concerned we didn't 'disarve wan ha'penny of it.'

The little note was the first item on the agenda that evening, so it was decided to make the old lady's place our first call. It upset our schedule a bit, but no matter.

The only light in her house was a very small paraffin lamp stood in a recess near the fireplace, augmented by the glow from the turf fire. While waiting for my cue, I remember watching the reflections from the fire dancing on the few bits of delft on the old dresser near the door. I played my Divil Doubt part in a low key, which I thought the occasion demanded. But when I got to the fireplace, the old lady rose from her chair and gave me a good hug. 'Good luck, boys, and God spare ye,' she called after us. It so happened we were the last rhymers she was to see. She passed away the following spring.

Sometimes we would be specially requested not to call at a particular house because of illness in the family. Such requests were usually accompanied by a larger donation than usual, mostly a half-crown. But to us it just meant that we could add an extra call to our schedule that evening. It might appear a bit ironic that we were getting more for a non-appearance than a full performance, but we never gave it a thought.

There was a special event to mark the end of the rhyming season: the Rhymers' dance, a much-publicised affair, with full refreshments laid on. For a week or two afterwards, when the result of some fund-raising event was being announced at Sunday Mass, ears would be strained to hear how much had been donated by the Christmas rhymers.

Our neighbourhood was always well blessed with a variety of fine amateur entertainers, in both song and dance. All were self-taught; none had had a professional lesson in their lives, which was probably the secret of their talents. Any attempt to professionalise would most probably have ruined those fine old arts, which were handed down from earlier generations. Some of the step dances were unique, like the 'Jug o' Punch', a combination of dance and verse. Each verse was followed by some very fancy footwork. The expert on this dance was Jimmy's Pat, who needed a considerable amount of encouragement – and probably a couple of half-ones – to get in the mood. But Pat's interpretation of the 'Jug' was worth waiting for. Then there was wee Barney Bogey; his speciality was 'Maggie Pickins'. This dance required basically the same expertise as the 'Jug' yet was different from it insofar as the dance and verse were performed simultaneously.

The hornpipe expert was Big Mickey's Joe, son of the Kinnego Band's famous bass drummer; this step dance was sometimes called the half-door hornpipe. In those days the doors of most houses were in two halves: the bottom half was always kept shut and, apart from providing something to lean on, it was very useful for keeping the hens out. In order to get the best effect from Joe's talent, the half-door would be removed and laid on the floor. Then Joe, all six foot and more of him, would give a renowned performance. I was always fascinated by this man, who always wore a double-breasted watch-chain. He always seemed to carry loose change in his pocket, and the jingle from the loose change and the watch-chain seemed to keep perfect time with his feet. Invariably these dancers would be wearing hobnailed boots, which on the floor seemed be as light as feathers. The non-specialist dances were the 'Set' and the 'Lancers' but the six- or eight-hand reel groups were in a class of their own. But you had to start off young to be a good dancer, and although the women didn't like dancing with 'weans', as they called us young ones, it was the only way to learn.

Of the many musicians, two were outstanding. Quentin of Crockahinney could play a melodeon from dusk till dawn without getting tired. Pat Mulhern was our renowned fiddler. This art varied considerably in the north and west of Ireland; some fiddles had more strings than others and were tuned differently. Pat Mulhern, however, was an acclaimed Donegal fiddler and was well worthy of the title.

We had many fine singers; this particular talent seemed to run in families. Singing, which was always performed without musical accompaniment, was a unique art. The Connor family in Effishabreda produced some fine performers. Annie Connor and her brother Dan were specialists: any musical gathering they attended was an assured success. Another good singer was a young man from Sledrin called Geordie Kelly. Not only did he have a fine voice but he also possessed a great repertoire of songs and ballads, such as 'Garryowen', 'Dark Rosaleen', 'The Bold Fenian Men', 'The Old Bog Road' and many others. Our ballads were usually about the patriot, the rebel, the exile or the emigrant; all were part of contemporary life, so we could easily identify with them. They were all part of the 'ould flame'. Kelly's most-requested ballad was a local one entitled 'Glenswilly'. It didn't rhyme very well, so the vowel was modified to 'Glen-su-lee'. It was the emigrant's lament, as this extract shows:

In Creeslough town my friends stood round,
My comrades kind and true.
And as I grasped each well-known hand
To bid each one adieu,
I said, 'Cheer up, my countrymen!

For soon you will be free
To raise the sun-burst proudly
O'er the hills of Glen-su-lee.'
May peace and plenty flow supreme
Along Lough Swilly shore.
May discord never enter the
Old homesteads any more.
And may the day soon come around
When I'll return to thee,
To live where my forefathers lived
And died, in Glen-su-lee.

Then we had Hughie-in-Point, a staunch Republican. Hughie didn't have much time for the romantic stuff; he left that to the sobsters. He liked to be associated with the patriots of the past, and they didn't come any greater than the famous John Mitchel. Hughie could put so much power behind this one, you could almost feel the thatch lifting from the roof:

I am a true-born Irishman,
John Mitchel is my name,
And for to join my countrymen
From Newry town I came.
I struggled hard both night and day
To free my native land,
For which I was transported
Unto Van Diemen's Land.

We also had a very tough football team. It didn't have a name; instead, it simply relied on its reputation. But it couldn't even afford a full set of kit – although that wasn't considered important. For those who couldn't afford the green-and-white-striped jersey and football boots, it was shirtsleeves, trouser bottoms tucked inside the socks, and a stout pair of hobnailed boots with steel toe-plates. John-in-the-Big-Hill was the goalkeeper; his brother Anton always played full-back. John always wore his cap back to front just for luck. On the wings were two of the fastest men ever seen on a football field: John James McCarron and Mickey the Fiddler. Mickey's other nickname, which he acquired on the football field, was Tipper-Up; this was because he was always telling the other players not to hang on to the ball in a tackle. Just lob it over the opponent's head, or 'Tip 'er up!' as he always shouted.

In the centre were men like Mickey Watt, Nealy Mc-Glinchey, Johnnie Fith, Owney in Bradfield, assisted by a Coyle, a Kelly or a Connor. The team never worried too much about fancy techniques; the modern television jargon about strikers and sweepers was unheard of. Every man in our team considered himself a striker and many an opposing goalkeeper got the shock of his life as the ball whizzed past his ear from nowhere. Sometimes there would be a fixture with an amateur club team from one of the towns. These posh teams with their fancy gear tended to look on our fellas with a certain amount of disdain, thinking, no doubt, that if we couldn't afford the proper gear then we couldn't be much of a team. However, by the time the final whistle blew, visitors had usually changed their minds. Having proper football gear just wasn't enough to stop a few determined men in hobnailed boots with steel toe-plates.

4

SARIDA

I had a big surprise when one day the family moved lock, stock and barrel from the Rock down to where my granny used to live, in Sarida. At the time I couldn't make out why this sudden move took place. But then wee fellas like me were seldom consulted on serious family matters of this kind. For some unexplained reason, granny's place hadn't been left to anyone when she died. It was a much better proposition than the Rock: the land was better – much easier to work – and there was more of it. Although I didn't know it at the time, the place was much sought after by others. Perhaps it was to forestall them that we moved in, because the place wasn't legally ours yet – not until the day it came up for sale by public auction. I felt very proud of my mother that day. I can see her now, dressed in her Sunday best and looking very determined, the only woman among a large gathering of men. Mind you, I would wince every time she nodded to the auction-eer, because each nod upped the price by another twenty pounds. Where under the sun is she going to find that kind of money? I kept saying to myself. The other bidders didn't know how determined she was to buy the place at any price. I gave a great sigh of relief when I heard Sarida being knocked down to her for the sum of three hundred pounds. And this at a time when even I knew she would be hard put to find three hundred pence.

Sarida, of course, was for her eldest son, James, who at the time was somewhere in the great US of A, trying to raise the three hundred pounds by the sweat of his brow – but more of that later. Meanwhile, the family was getting down to the business of settling in. Now we had more of a spread than most of the neighbours, since we could use the Rock land for grazing. I don't know how James viewed the situation, because he was now faced with the same old problem. The rest of us would have to go before he could really call the place his own. But the family was already breaking up; my two eldest sisters were already married, with families of their own. As for the rest of us, it was merely a question of time.

Amidst all our trials and tribulations, the life cycle continued as always: births, deaths and marriages. The marrying age was much higher than now and was determined by domestic circumstances. The man of the family, to whom the holding had been bequeathed, had to wait until the rest of the family had dispersed. The women had to wait until they were asked or, more importantly, until their parents were asked: parents' consent was all-important. Courtship was not considered to be an essential formality to marriage in those days. When a man considered himself free to marry, he might first of all send his best friend to the home of the prospective bride to find out if his intentions would be welcome. Many men, however, when the urge was on them, would waive this brief preliminary. With a bottle of whiskey and accompanied by a friend, the man in search of a wife would simply call at homes where daughters of marriageable age were available. Once the bottle was placed in the centre of the table, no further request was needed; the bottle was the spirit of the occasion.

If there was more than one girl available, all that was left for the father to say was 'Which wan did ye have yer eye on?' Generally speaking, the man wanting to take a wife on board didn't have to search too far. Most likely, he would be accepted at the first house he called at. The passage of time has eroded many of the old customs associated with weddings, more's the pity. It was the advent of the motor car that brought about most changes. When the horse and sidecar was the chief mode of conveyance, people had more time to 'burn a bottle', which was a very ancient custom. Even in those days there was a certain amount of 'keeping up with the Joneses' to be observed. Indeed, if my memory serves me right, there were some people who believed they *were* the Joneses. Two sidecars to a wedding was about average; if there were three or more, then it was hailed as a big wedding. But with four passengers on each sidecar and a driver on the 'dicky' and a bow or two of white ribbon on the horse's harness, a wedding was a wedding whatever its size. As far as us boys were concerned, it mattered not who was marrying whom, or why, providing we were neighbours or relatives and thus qualified for an invitation. For high on the menu was sure to be boiled beef, with lovely barley soup. Since Christmas Day was the only day in the year when we would be likely to get beef, weddings were occasions not to be missed.

The marriage ceremony took place early in the morning at Cockhill Chapel; the wedding party would then repair to some public house in Buncrana which catered for such events. It would be late evening, and long dark, when the wedding party returned to the bride's home, where all the jollifications were held. As the wedding party entered the bride's townland, it was time for the neighbours to show their appreciation of the event. The countryside became floodlit as trusses of straw, known as battles, which had been husbanded all day near the fire to make sure they were dry, were set alight and held high in the air on pitchforks. At the bride's home, two battles would be set alight – one for the bride and one for the groom. This was our way of saying long life and happiness to the newly wedded pair. It was also the custom for a group of local young men to meet the wedding party and escort it on the last stage of the journey home. But when motor cars became the fashion, this old custom had to be abandoned also.

The young men who made up the escort would not leave the premises until they had toasted the health of the newly-weds. So the best man's first duty was to fill a jug with whiskey and take it out to the uninvited guests. Even then some of those characters would insist on 'wan for the road'. The thatched roofs were very low and it was no problem to hoist some blithe spirit onto the roof; he would then crawl along to the chimney and lower an empty bottle on the end of a piece of string. Although this was a tricky operation because of the fire, the best man had no option but to fill the bottle and watch it disappear up the chimney. Then, and only then, would the escort disappear also, and the jollifications proper could begin.

So it was eating, drinking, dancing and singing until daylight. The following night was 'bottle-drink' night, when every neighbour and well-wisher would bring a bottle of whiskey (mostly home-made) and the entertainment of the previous night would be repeated. Honeymoons weren't the fashion in those days; the Sunday following a wedding was known as Outgoing Sunday. The newly married couple would attend mass at Cockhill, where they would receive congratulations from all who knew them. This was another occasion for a 'big night'. Small wonder, then, that weddings were looked upon as important events in the social calendar. For all the marriages, however, the old matriarchal system was still very much in evidence. There were many cases of a son being left with a widowed mother, and the old lady would never allow a strange woman to live under her roof, if she could help it. So by the time the son had the place to himself, he was too old and had lost the notion of marriage altogether. This system was no doubt the cause of the large population of old bachelors and was sadly reflected in other ways throughout Inishowen. Many of the old buildings became derelict. There are many old houses where in days of yore large families were raised; now only the four walls of such houses remain. These old places are being lost without trace as the forestry commission moves in. The long, regimental lines of spruce are a poor substitute for what used to be.

As with weddings, deaths were also occasions of special significance, although we never treated them with the same sombreness as prevails in other lands. To us, death was but a step to eternal life, and regardless of in what circumstances it took place among us, it was always considered to be 'the will of God'. Whether everyone accepted the validity of this statement or not, there was no doubt that it softened the blow for many. But it must be said that there were far too many occasions when we passed on to God responsibility which was rightly ours. In cases of accident or sudden illness, we always sent for the priest first, not the doctor. At first sight, it would appear that we were more concerned with the spiritual, rather than the temporal, welfare of the sick. This wasn't true in all cases; the doctor's fee for a visit was ten shillings and not every family had that kind of money available for emergencies. Doctors would not accept 'I'll see ye agin' – the local parlance for paying later – they wanted their fee on the spot.

The priest, however, had more authority. A messenger would go to Buncrana with a request for the priest to visit a sick person. When the priest returned, he would give the messenger a note to take to the doctor. This practice was called 'getting a line', which guaranteed that the doctor would be reimbursed from the funds of some local charity. Because of this slow procedure, there must have been many occasions when medical attention arrived too late. In many cases, then, poverty denied us the right to choose between the priest and the doctor. Even today, Inishowen has only one hospital, at Carndonagh; the next-nearest is at Letterkenny, west of Lough Swilly. But the community has the benefit of an up-to-date health service. No such facilities existed in the old days.

When death occurred, the whole neighbourhood shared the sorrow. The neighbours would visit the house of the deceased to pray and offer condolences to the bereaved family, with the greeting 'I'm sorry for yer trouble.' This custom still prevails and no doubt will forever. At night the young people would attend the wake and stay until daylight. Clay pipes would be kept filled and passed round at intervals among the men, while the women were offered snuff. Wakes were great occasions for storytelling, mostly ghost stories. For a while after a wake, I would be too scared to venture out after dark, unless our old dog Nettle came along to keep me company. But, like all dogs, Nettle would dash off somewhere into the darkness, only to come bounding over a ditch later, landing at my feet and scaring the living daylights out of me.

There were no hearses in those days and coffins would be carried on the shoulders of four men for long distances over rough roads in all weathers. It would be the job of someone to cast an eye over the followers and sort out groups of four who would be roughly the same height. By the time the funeral reached Cockhill, every man attending would have helped to carry the coffin. Maybe this was why only men attended funerals. There was some very important protocol to be observed at funerals also. Men who were closest relatives would carry the coffin from the deceased's house to the boundary of his land. They would lead the cortège all the way to the chapel gates and carry the remains into the chapel – and, after the service, on to the graveside. This custom prevails to this day, and is known as 'the first and last lift'.

The old custom of collecting 'offerings' at funerals has long been abandoned. The purpose of offerings was to cover the cost of saying Mass for the repose of the souls of the dead. But it was never explained why this particular holy function cost extra money. Eventually, like everything else where money is the criterion, offerings became a kind of status symbol. The amounts donated varied; there was no fixed sum. Close relatives were expected to put a pound per household on the table, while five or ten shillings from relatives outside the family was normal. For the neighbours, donations of a half-crown to a shilling were about average. It was important, however, to have your name called out when your donation was being collected. Generally, those who made the biggest donation got the loudest shout. In cases where the deceased had been a local notable or had been a doer of worthy deeds, offerings could reach the sum of twenty-five pounds or more. In this event, the officiating clergy would eulogise more than somewhat. But on many occasions when the deceased was the last of a family, with no relatives left to mourn, and the offerings came to a few pounds, there would be no eulogy. Instead, there were just a few hurried 'Our Father's and 'Hail Mary's. From this, then, it seemed that the repose of one's soul depended very much on one's status in society.

As mentioned earlier, ghost stories were always very popular among us. They were part of the folklore and the more they made our hair stand on end the better we liked them. Eventually we got our own ghost, because if all ghost stories are true, every self-respecting community has had one at one time or another. Ours was a harmless enough phenomenon, taking the form of a light which kept appearing and disappearing at intervals on the same piece of ground for four or five years, until it finally disappeared for good. I can vouch for at least three sightings; each time, however, I was left wondering did I see the light or didn't I? It moved so fast it was a case of 'Now you see me, now you don't.' It always kept to the same course, sometimes appearing as a pale yellow light travelling at running speed. Other times it would be a bright blue light travelling at meteoric speed for three or four hundred yards before disappearing. Some of the wise men in the locality believed that it was caused by an iron-ore deposit in the area. The outcrop can cause a glow in the dark that is sometimes called wildfire. It can cling to the fur of a hare or rabbit and give the impression of a light. But even they had to admit that no animal could travel at such speed.

My brother always claimed to be the only man to have had a close encounter with the light; further, he could prove that he was stone-cold sober at the time. He was cycling past the light's territory in the very early hours of the morning when a stone from the rough road caused his bicycle to shed its chain. This could not have happened at a worse time or place for poor Charley. He was bent down, fiddling about in the dark, trying to get the chain back on its sprocket, when, lo and behold, a pool of yellow light appeared about fifty yards from the yard. Seated in the centre of the lighted area was a woman, calmly combing her long tresses of hair. She was talking to someone else, although no other body was visible. As soon as the chain was back on its sprocket, Charley didn't hang about awaiting further developments. Afterwards, he was prepared to wager that he had set a new world record for his speed over the last stretch home. As time went by, the presence of the light was taken for granted. 'Have ye seen the light lately?' became a normal conversational remark.

In the end, two or three of the senior locals decided that the matter was serious enough for closer investigation. They went to the clergy to see if they could throw any further light on the matter. The clergy listened very attentively to the men's story before asking them if they were certain they had seen a light. Two of the men were positive they had but the other one wasn't quite sure. The clergy wanted to know if the light had interfered with anyone or caused any annoyance; the men had to admit that it hadn't. In that case, the clergy advised, the men should ignore the light and let it get on with its business, and in due course it would disappear. This was precisely what happened. Before the light finally disappeared, however, I was to have another sighting; but the occasion was so special to me personally that I will come back to it later.

5
—

'KENT-MEN', THE FLU AND HOT SERMONS

As well as food shortages caused by the war, clothes were also a problem – when we could afford any, which wasn't often. Probably the men fared a bit better in this respect, especially if they could manage to earn a couple of pounds extra at the Scotch harvest. The blue serge suit was the most fashionable in those days. Mind you, it had to last a long time; in time, the nap would all be brushed away and the seat of the trousers would become very shiny. But, providing there were no holes in it, even when threadbare it was still a Sunday suit. The women and children, however, had to make do with reach-me-downs from the 'kent-men's' stalls. Besides second-hand bargains, for anyone wanting an hour's free entertainment the place to head for was the market square in Buncrana on a fair day. There all the 'kent-men' would be gathered and, having laid out their stalls, they would proceed to compete with each other in extolling the virtues of their wares.

The most interesting character among them that I recall was one Barney McIver, salesman, showman, comedian and singer, all rolled into one. Although the little wooden sign above his stall simply said 'Ladies & Gents Outfitter, Second-hand Ward-robes a Speciality', Barney's stall always attracted the biggest crowd. Many were on the lookout for a bargain, and many just to hear the craic. Having laid his wares out to the best possible advantage, Barney would then adorn himself with the trappings of his trade. These were a length of very fine suit material, which he draped around his shoulders, and a tape measure. The suit material was Barney's main prop and was used strictly for advertisement purposes. The makings of a suit for a man or a woman was on offer for £3 but it was doubtful if Barney would have parted with any of the material, even if an offer was made. Nobody could afford new suits and, after all, selling second-hand clothes was what he was there for.

He would keep a sharp lookout for people making their way back from the Pound Lane, where all the animals were bought and sold. Barney had an uncanny knack for selecting potential customers. If they had a spare pound in their pockets, Barney could almost smell it. He always made a great play for the ladies; in this respect, it was said he could charm the birds from the bushes with his: 'Ah good woman. Will ye come 'ere a minit! Come and see yer Uncle Barney.' When the selected victim had edged her way to Barney's stall, she would be greeted with: 'Begod, yer a fine-looking woman. Tell me, how come a fine figure of a woman like yerself got hooked up with that ould wrack of a man you've got there for a husband.' The lady's husband, of course, would be waiting on the edge of the crowd, looking rather sheepish but nevertheless enjoying the craic. The lady herself soon warmed to Barney's flattery and didn't mind acting as his model. 'Now if you had married me,' Barney would continue, 'not only would you be Mrs McIver but the best-dressed woman in the whole of Ireland. Wait till ye see this,' he would say as he draped the length of suiting on the lady. Then, turning to the crowd, he would shout: 'There ye are. Wouldn't she look great, dressed in the finest piece of worsted iver to lave the shores of England? And all jist for three pound.' At this point Barney, if the mood was on him, would introduce a verse from one of the old romantics. Smoothing the drape round the lady, he would burst forth with:

Her claspened dress
Was softly flowing down.
Oh, I'll love ye evermore,
Sweet colleen of the shore,
My true love,
My snowy-breasted pearl.

Heady stuff this, but the lady and the crowd enjoyed it. Now it was time for business. Barney would continue with: 'It doesn't look like thon ould fella of yours is going to spend three pound on ye the day. Never mind, maybe some ither time. But niver let it be said that Barney McIver would let any woman leave his stall without a bargain.' Reaching to the back, he would then produce a nice two-piece, shouting: 'Don't worry, I'm not going to charge ye three pounds. I'm not even going to charge ye fifty bob. I'm damned if I'm even going to charge ye two pound. But yer a fine-looking woman and a sport. It's yours for thirty bob and it's the finest bargain in the market this day.'

Some of the old stagers knew that the most likely time for a good bargain was when the 'kent-men' were packing their unsold wares back in the hampers ready to go home. Our old friend Hughdie's Willie was a firm believer in this policy. A good pair of ex-army britches was all Willie ever bothered about. He and Barney knew each other well and many a battle of wits took place between them over the years, with Willie usually winning in the end. Barney would be busy re-packing his hampers when he would spot Willie hanging around the stall. All of a sudden, a pair of army britches would be held up in the air. 'What the hell do I want these things for?' Barney would shout. 'Who'll give me three and a tanner for them quick, before I put them away?' 'Half a crown,' Willie would offer from somewhere in the crowd. Completely ignoring Willie, Barney would shout: 'Will somebody give me three bob quick before I change my mind?' 'Half a crown,' Willie would offer. 'Has any of you miserable lot got two and ninepence on ye?' 'Half a crown,' Willie would repeat once more. Barney knew no one was going to bid against Willie, so he just carried on as if Willie didn't exist, and pretended to put the britches back in the hamper. Instead, he would roll them up in a tight bundle and, swinging round, would aim it straight at Willie's head. 'Gimme yer half-crown, ye miserable ould skinflint, ye! If I wusn't in a hurry to get home for me tay . . . You'd niver fart in 'em for that kind of money!' was Barney's final comment. Normally, a pair of leggings, or puttees, was the proper accessory to go with a pair of britches, but Willie never bothered with these extras. A couple of strips cut from an old meal-bag and wound round the tops of his boots did Willie just as well. Maybe that was why some people called him 'Soger's Willie'.

By the time the war ended, we had lost interest in it – and in the politicians of the time. We had enough pain and sorrow of our own to contend with. We had been visited by a plague: a killer virus which the medical authorities couldn't diagnose. Even if they could, there were no medicines or facilities to deal with it. They called it influenza but to us it was just 'the flu'. The young adult and middle-aged groups seemed to bear the brunt of it. I can recall the rest of our family being dangerously ill, some of them delirious for days. Yet my father and I never suffered from as much as a cold throughout. Yet you could be speaking to someone today, who seemed fit and well, and the next day be terribly shocked to hear they were dead. There were no effective medicines that we knew of, and the local doctor was at his wits' end trying to cope with the situation. Then someone discovered that 'wee-still' whiskey, taken as hot punch, would stave off the worst ravages of the disease. But there weren't enough fit men around to make the stuff, so it was in short supply. Although 'wee-still' was always being denounced from every pulpit in the land, there was no doubt it saved many lives during the big flu.

My dear mother's greatest worry was for James in America. Irish immigrants were now being drafted for the war. Having secured her father's holding, her dearest wish was to see James return safely to Sarida. Alas, it was not to be, for at precisely 11 am on 11 November 1918, just as the first siren announced the end of the war that was to end all wars, her coffin was lowered to her grave at Cockhill. Aged fifty-five, she left a gap that was never filled.

About that time, Master Kearney in his wisdom decided that I was proficient enough in Latin and liturgical phrases to become an altar boy at Cockhill – 'clarking', as we called it. The incumbent clergy at the time were Fathers Doherty, O'Kane and Agnew. Father Doherty was the parish priest; he was a big man and a powerful orator. When it was time for his Sunday sermon, off would come his chasuble and, rolling up his sleeves, he would stride towards the pulpit. The congregation would brace itself for the verbal storm that was to follow. Everyone would soon be reminded of their failure to live up to the standard their religion demanded. We 'clarks' lolled about on the safe side of the altar rails, hoping he didn't mean us. His recurring theme, of course, was the evil 'poteen'. His campaign to stamp it out went on for a number of years and had some far-reaching effects. But more about that later. Meanwhile, as far as we 'clarkers' were concerned, Father Doherty was by no means our greatest affliction: it was the senior boy in charge who tended to make life difficult. A good thump or a hefty kick was the sort of punishment he meted out for any laxity in devotional duties. He was a very superior person indeed, and it was clear from the cut of his jib that he was a man destined for higher things. Indeed, he went on to become an eminent theologian and a bishop.

6
—

BLACK AND TANS

It was an exciting time for us boys: so much was happening or about to happen that we never knew what to expect next. A wave of political fervour gripped the land and, although we youngsters didn't understand why, our lack of knowledge didn't curb our excitement. For how were we to know that the ashes of Easter 1916 were still smouldering and ready to burst into flames any minute? Some of the signs, however, were so ominous that they just couldn't be ignored. Our old national standard, the Green Flag, with the harp surmounted by the crown, was having to make way for our new colours, the green, white and orange of the Tricolour, which now fluttered over all political gatherings. The first post-war general election had taken place and Sinn Féin had entered the political arena for the first time. But never before had a political party entered a general-election contest with so many disadvantages as did Sinn Féin in 1918. At least 50 per cent of its candidates were either in jail and internment camps or on the run. In the circumstances, the party had to rely on its manifesto, and the message had to be loud and clear. First and foremost, Ireland was a nation of thirty-two counties and its people were a distinct race, having a distinct culture. Ireland was a separate land mass; it never was, and never would be, a part of Britain. The seat of its own government would be Dublin, not Westminster. Its first task would be to put Ireland's case for self-determination before an international jury, the World Peace Conference, which was held in Paris.

The election results were astounding. Sinn Fein swept the board, winning 80 per cent of the seats. Only around the Ulster border was the old Nationalist party (the Home Rulers) able to hang on by the skin of its teeth, with greatly reduced majorities. So the nation's will had been declared, but to start with it had to be a government *in absentia*. We had to wait until many of its leaders had been released or had escaped from jail. When the first cabinet of the new Dáil Éireann was formed, only essential portfolios were allocated. The names of the holders, however, were to become internationally famous later: Éamon de Valera (president), Count Plunkett (foreign affairs), Michael Collins (finance), Cathal Brugha (defence), and Richard Mulcahy (chief of staff). The first reaction of the British government was predictable enough: the Irish election and its new government were declared illegal. Meanwhile, the Irish government set about implementing one of the main planks in its election platform. It would proceed to place Ireland's case for self-determination before the World Peace Conference. There couldn't be any logical argument against this line of approach but, as history has proved many times before and since, logic may be a useful aid to understanding your world, but something positive is needed to change it. After all, the war to end all wars had just ended. Millions of men laid down their lives on the battlefields of Europe in defence of the rights of small nations to determine their own destiny. And Ireland, per capita, made a contribution of equal measure to that aim, as did any of the other participants. No one could argue with the fact that Ireland was a small nation and all set fair to seek self-determination by the ballot, not the bullet.

Perhaps we were a bit naive in thinking that, since President Woodrow Wilson was the dominant figure at the Peace Conference, the old American connection might come to our aid. It soon became evident, however, that strong moves were afoot to block Ireland's admission to the conference. The steering committee refused to grant credentials to the men of Dáil Éireann and ruled that Ireland was outside the terms of reference of the conference and constituted purely a domestic matter for Britain. So our three delegates, Éamon de Valera, Arthur Griffiths and Count Plunkett, had to unpack their bags, and our first attempt to break bread at the table of the great democracies came to nothing. Britain, having now secured the blessing of the conference, proceeded to clear up the mess in her backyard. In the traditional manner, and with vigour, she applied herself to the task of imposing a military situation on what was clearly a major political problem. Soon Ireland was living under siege conditions, with over 50,000 troops deployed throughout the land and a top army general in command. Our old home-grown force, the Royal Irish Constabulary, was relieved of its civilian command and another army general put in charge.

The police now carried rifles as well as batons, and in effect became a complete paramilitary force. In this manner Britain battened down the hatches and prepared to ride out the storm as the War of Independence got under way.

Up until then, our relations with the 'sogers', as we called the army, was reasonably cordial. Buncrana had long been a garrison town; for as long as I could remember, there had been a permanent military camp between Fahan and Buncrana, while a few miles north there was a military installation at Dunree Fort. The local shopkeepers did a considerable amount of trade with the army, so our attitude was one of ambivalence based on an attitude of: 'You mind your business and I'll mind mine.' Of course, at that time the role of the army was confined to guarding the Western approaches. As soon as it was called to the aid of the civil power and became part of the forces of repression, attitudes changed dramatically.

Fortunately, we did have men of vision who had foreseen that the situation now confronting us would inevitably come. For decades we had been 'politicking' about Home Rule and had got nowhere. Now there was only one choice left: if we wanted independence, we would have to fight for it. But how, and with what, was the problem, remembering that Britain had all advantages in men and material, while we didn't have enough resources to 'poke the lion's tail', never mind tackle him head-on. What we did have were many good men, languishing in the jails and internment camps of Britain from as far back as Easter 1916. It was in such places that the cutting edge of our fighting forces was honed and the nucleus of one of the most dedicated and disciplined of paramilitary forces yet known – the Irish Republican Army – was formed. But an army has to have firearms; the only way to get any was to go out and capture them. Thus the barracks and armouries of the RIC became the main targets. This force had long ceased to be the old civilian body we once knew; its main role now was to act as the eyes and ears of British intelligence. Raids and ambushes became almost a daily or nightly occurrence, as did the shootings and killings. This was a guerrilla war for which Britain, for all her preponderance of resources, had no answer. The IRA was deployed in very small groups that could move fast, strike hard and melt back into the countryside. The Crown forces would reply with wide swoops and mass arrests, which only added fuel to the flames.

Soon it was evident that the RIC was losing both its grip and its nerve. There were rumours of resignations. Meanwhile, Britain was busy recruiting a new force to deal with the deteriorating situation – a body imbued with a new sense of aggressiveness. This new force was designed to tighten the screw and at the same time boost the flagging spirit of the RIC. I well remember the day Charley Blue the postman came on his round in a terrible hurry, eager to spread the news that the Black and Tans had arrived in Buncrana. Two other wee fellas and myself set off immediately to see them, running most of the way. We were so excited, thinking we were going to see black men for the first time. How deeply disappointed we were to discover, after running all that way, that the Black and Tans were only ordinary white men after all. It was from their uniforms that they gained their title, not the colour of their skin. Compared with the police and soldiers we had been accustomed to, this new force looked very odd indeed. They wore long black paramatta coats over army uniforms, with Tam-o'-shanters without badges for head-gear. With rifles slung over their shoulders, they patrolled the main street of Buncrana in pairs.

A considerable number of the force were Ulstermen but the main body was recruited in England. Its enhanced rates of pay – ten shillings per day, rising to four pounds fifteen per week – made many a long-serving RIC man turn green with envy. The strange thing was that the man commanding the force wasn't even an Englishman; he was a Canadian, going by the name of Sir Hamar Greenwood. So it wasn't long before ballads were on the streets, telling about the doings of Hamar Greenwood's men.

The new force soon got down to business; its main preoccupation seemed to be a campaign of provocation, and harassment of the civilian population. They would race round the countryside, at any hour of the day or night, in semi-armoured vehicles, with wire wheels, known as Crossley tenders. It became very dangerous to meet them on the narrow roads with a horse and cart. Horses were not used to the noise of motors in those days, and the Tans would approach with all the speed and noise their vehicles could produce. The horse would rear up and invariably the cart and its owner would finish up in the ditch. There would be loud cheers from the Tans as they raced past, sometimes firing a couple of rounds into the air just for the hell of it. At other times they would go round the houses, arresting every young man they came across; then they would take them away, hold them for a few days and release them. It seemed to be a kind of numbers game for propaganda purposes; the Tans wanted to show that, by arresting so many people, they were earning their ten bob a day.

At that time, of course, County Donegal was still an integral part of the province of Ulster, which was about the only part of Ireland where the king's writ still ran. Most of the insurgent activity was around Dublin and in the south. Because of our geographical position, the activities of our local Volunteer force were somewhat inhibited and were mainly confined to disrupting communications. Cutting telephone lines, sawing down telephone poles and digging trenches across roads seemed to be the Volunteers' main activity. Sometime such tactics tended to be counter-productive. The Tans now carried a couple of stout planks in their Crossleys, and when they encountered a trench across the road, they bridged it with the planks and took the trench in their stride. It was when they had time on their hands to go round the houses, collect all the men they could find and stand over them with guns at the ready while the trench was filled in again that road-trenching went out of favour.

Then there was the time when an unsuccessful attempt was made to blow up one of the arches of Drumidirra bridge. Enough damage was done to make the bridge declared unfit for traffic. So now all traffic – mainly horses and carts – had to make a long detour up to the Rock and round by Kinnego in order to reach the main road again. The road up to the Rock was private property and very soon it got into a bad state of repair. The owner, Pat's

Daniel, complained to Big Phil, the local Volunteer commander, demanding that the road be repaired. Phil had no option but to commandeer every horse and cart in the locality, and their owners; they had to spend the best part of a day carting stones and gravel to fill in the ruts on the road to the Rock. This led to much acrimony about who should be responsible for maintaining the road. So our War for Independence seemed to be all right, as long as it didn't inconvenience anyone too much.

Sadly, for some of us wee boys, insurgent operations generally took place at night, when we were in bed. Had we known where and when things were happening, I'm sure we would have got there somehow. But we were lucky one morning to have a close-up of a daylight operation. For some reason, neither Master Kearney nor Miss Curran arrived at their normal time; this was most unusual for them. The scholars were chasing each other round the playground when suddenly everything went quiet, as someone shouted: 'Come and look at these men. They've got guns.' We all crowded round the gate, trying to get a glimpse at half a dozen armed men as they passed the school in single file. I was very surprised to see that two of the men were very close neighbours of ours – the last men in the world we would think of as being members of the insurgent movement. They all carried rifles and canvas-coloured bandoliers, and two of the party even wore the old slouch hats, reminiscent of the days of James Connolly's Citizen Army. They all looked very serious and ignored us onlookers entirely as they hurried towards the nearby railway line.

The first train of the day from Derry to Carndonagh

was just pulling out of Ballymagan station. Great plumes of white smoke drifted skywards as the train made its way along an area called the Drim. Then one of the raiders took up position between the rails and began to wave a red flag. At first it looked as if the train wasn't going to stop, and we were getting quite concerned about the man with the red flag. Then all of a sudden, amidst a shower of sparks and a great clatter, the train screeched to a halt. The man with the red flag stood his ground. Two of the party kept the driver covered as the other four went to the rear of the train; two of them boarded the guard's van, while the remaining two stood guard. Next we saw all the mailbags being tossed out onto the bank. The whole operation took less than five minutes; then the train, with much huffing and puffing, set off once more for its next stop, the Mentiaghs. The raiders shared out the mailbags between them and headed for the hills. The next issue of the *Derry Journal* carried a banner headline that read: 'Mail Train. Daring Hold-Up.'

7

AUXIES AND BALLADS

Throughout the rest of the country shootings, murders and reprisals continued with increasing ferocity. The Black and Tans were now a law unto themselves. Although public outcry against their activities continued to grow, the British government didn't want to know about the situation. It was only when a top army general threatened to resign unless the Tans were brought under control that the government began to take notice. A new bill was introduced under the Restoration of Order in Ireland Act; it was an enabling bill for the recruitment of another new force. The official title of this new body was the Auxiliaries, soon to be known as the 'Auxies'. It was an elite organisation open to ex-officers only; the first qualification for candidates was that they had previously held a commission in the army. Thus specially selected and trained, its first task was to restore discipline to the badly demoralised ranks of the Black and Tans. It was given a free hand to engage in a search-and-destroy mission, and so bring a final solution to the problem of Ireland. In practice this meant: 'Shoot first and ask questions later!' Its rate of pay was one pound per day plus allowances.

The house searches were usually carried out in the early hours of the morning: surprise was the main tactic employed. The Crossleys would be parked away in some quiet lane; then the Tans, with the Auxies in charge, would proceed in small groups on foot. Early one morning we were rudely awakened by a loud crash on the door, and a voice shouted: 'Open up!' This was immediately followed by: 'Open up or we'll break it down!' My father managed to get to the door before the threat was carried out. Even so, things got off to a very bad start. There was always an old wooden tub lying about outside; it was used for animal feed. That morning, for some reason or other, the tub had been left nearer the door than usual – a silly place to put it – and maybe I was the culprit. However, it had been raining hard during the night, so the old tub had collected a considerable amount of rainwater. As my father snatched the door open, an old towel that hung behind it blew outwards. The first reaction of one of the visitors was to jump backwards, finishing up on his backside in the tub, which was half full of water. Not the sort of welcome to put a member of the Crown's forces in a good humour.

Anyway, in they came. The room door was wide open and, although I was trembling under the blankets, I could hear their strange English voices. There seemed to be just two of them, flashing their torches round the kitchen, where two of my sisters occupied the big bed. 'Hullo! Who have we here?' I heard one of the men say. Now I became really apprehensive. The elder of the two girls was always considered to be very outspoken. Were she foolish enough to make a wrong remark to these fellas, particularly the one who had sat in the tub, there was no telling how they might react.

'What's the weather like?' I heard her ask.

'For your information, it's pissing down, which pleases you, I expect, knowing we're out in it,' one of them replied. 'Now then, let's have less cheek and some information, if you don't mind. You attend all the dances around here. When did you last see so-and-so? How about so-and-so? Seen him lately?'

I heard my sister say that the last she had heard of one young man, he was in Scotland; otherwise, all her answers were negative. What was amazing, however, was how extremely well informed the Auxies were. They knew not only the names but also the nicknames of many of the activists in the area.

'How many sons have you got?' I heard my father being asked.

'Three,' he replied.

'Where are they?'

'One in America and one in Scotland; the other one is in his bed down in the room there,' he told them.

Both men now entered the room. Although pretending to be asleep, I was wide awake, watching their torch-beams darting about in the darkness. 'How old is this one?' a strange voice asked; at the same time the blankets were flicked from my head.

'Twelve,' my father replied.

'He's big for a twelve-year-old,' said the stranger.

At the same time I could feel the cold steel of a revolver-muzzle being pressed not too gently into the side of my now-sweating forehead. Maybe it was only kept there for a second but to me it was an eternity.

'What's that contraption?' the other man asked, having spotted the old spinning wheel with his torch-beam.

The old wheel had been in the family for generations and always stood in the corner. 'It's a spinning wheel,' my father replied.

'That's what you tell us; it could be a machine-gun, for all we know. Get it out and let's have a look,' the man ordered.

My father lifted the old spinning wheel and placed it in the centre of the floor. As the two men examined the old wheel I noticed that, as well as hand guns, each of them had a rifle slung over his shoulder. As they turned to go, I heard one of them mutter something which sounded like 'Bloody rubbish.' Whereupon he gave the wheel a hefty kick, sending it flying against the wall, where the old pedal fell off.

'What did you say your name was?' my father was asked.

When he told them, one of them said, 'All right, Devlin! Maybe you'll have some information for us next time we call.'

It was now clear enough for them to see that we still had a small stack of hay in the garden. 'You've still got some hay left then,' one of them remarked. Then to his partner he said jokingly: 'That stuff makes a great bonfire, you know.'

The house was still reeking of whiskey and cigar smoke long after they had gone. And so, to this day, I've only to put my nose inside a pub – which isn't often – and I get an immediate flashback to that spring morning so long ago, when we were hosts to the Tans and the Auxies.

Nettle, our old dog, let us down badly; normally she could hear footsteps a long way off and would keep barking until all was clear. That particular night she never made a whimper; as soon as the visitors had left, she crept from under a bed with a querulous look on her face. Have they gone? she seemed to ask. So maybe a dog's sense of smell is as good as its hearing when there are nasty men with guns around. When day cleared we discovered that there must have been more than two visitors: we went to the barn and found all our seedcorn and potatoes strewn on the floor. The potatoes had been smashed to pulp, having been trodden on by army boots. The seedcorn had been emptied on top and the little bit of fodder we had been saving was strewn everywhere. The place was in a shambles.

I was to have one more close encounter with the Auxies the following spring. That was the day my brother Charley and I set off for the Isle of Inch with a load of turf. It had been a bad harvest: fodder was scarce, and we were hoping to barter the turf for a few bales of straw to tide us over until the spring grass came again. We got as far as Fahan on the Derry road; at a place called 'the Chains' there was a roadblock, and sandbags and barbed-wire entanglements left just enough room for a horse and cart to pass. Two fully armed soldiers manned the roadblock. They stopped us and told us we would have to wait. From a nearby house which was being used as a military post, an Auxie appeared and strolled towards us.

'What have you got on board?' he asked.

'Turf,' Charley told him.

'I can see that. But what have you got underneath?' Then he nodded to the soldiers, who climbed on the cartwheels and proceeded to prod the turf with their bayonets, scattering most of the load on the road.

After a while, one of the soldiers looked at the Auxie and shook his head, indicating that there was nothing in the cart but turf. 'All right, make the buggers up-end it,' the Auxie ordered. He wanted the load emptied on the road.

But, as luck would have it, someone at the post, obviously with more authority, shouted: 'Get that lot on the move. They're blocking the road.' Charley and I were now scrambling around, trying to get the scattered turf back on the cart. We threw them on any old how; we would rebuild the load once we were out of harm's way.

'All right! On your way!' the bold Auxie ordered. Whereupon he snatched a rifle from one of the soldiers and, holding it like a cricket bat, swung it with all the force he could muster. There was a dull, sickening thud as the rifle-butt landed on the mare's belly. Taken unawares, the poor old beast gave out an agonised groan as she almost slumped to the ground. She carried the mark of her encounter with the Auxie – a large lump on her side – for many weeks afterwards.

Down the centuries, balladry and recitation have always been closely associated with historical events in Ireland. The midwife to many of these renderings has always been times of trouble, and the 1920s were no exception. A ballad about someone or some event appeared almost weekly. For the price of one penny, we could sing the praises of our latest heroes, and likewise cherish the memory of our latter-day martyrs. For us youngsters, Kevin Barry topped the list, but there were many others, such as Sean McEoin, Sean Tracey, Dan Breen, Barry's flying column and many others. When we had exhausted all these, we could always fall back on that old evergreen, the Legion of the Rearguard.

I don't think we fully appreciated just what a powerful propaganda weapon the ballad was. Indeed, the British authorities treated them far more seriously than we did. To them it was seditious literature, and anyone found in possession of these little pennyworths was promptly arrested and interned. Mountjoy Jail in Dublin was the setting for many of the tragic events of that time; it had achieved far greater notoriety than the dreaded H-Blocks of the Maze Prison today. Because of particular circumstances, the memories of some of the tragic deaths, especially those of Thomas Ashe and Kevin Barry, lasted longer in the public mind than others. In his demand for prisoner-of-war status, Thomas Ashe went on hunger strike. The authorities, in an attempt to break him, resorted to that diabolical form of punishment, forcible feeding. As a consequence, Ashe died. It was nothing new for us young ones to have seen an animal that had broken into a potato pit and choked itself to death with a large spud in its throat. So we didn't have to stretch our imaginations too far to visualise a human being having a length of rubber tubing forced down his throat. Public indignation at the outrage forced an autopsy to be carried out. The coroner's jury gave a verdict of death from heart failure and congestion of the lungs. It also added a rider, condemning the practice of forcible feeding as inhuman.

There were so many contradictory reports about Kevin Barry's involvement in the struggle that you paid your

penny and took your choice. It was his age that caught
our imagination most and held our attention longest: he
was barely eighteen. The official account of his involvement was that he was found hiding underneath a
bread van in an area where an ambush had taken place
and a solider had been killed. He was charged on a
confession which he swore on affidavit had been beaten
out of him at the police station. The long legal debate
about the validity of the procedure under which he was
charged produced nothing. Barry was sentenced to death
by hanging, not by firing squad, the usual procedure at
the time. So, in spite of all the mercy pleas from home
and abroad, and amid protests and demonstrations, Barry
died on the gallows in November 1920. But in ballad and
recitation he remained with us for many years afterwards.

Although the war still raged, a fresh spate of rumours
was now afoot. It was taking Charley Blue the best part
of the day to complete his rounds because everybody was
anxious to hear the latest news. The gist of the rumours
was that an Australian prelate had taken on the task of
setting up a dialogue between London and Dublin. It
wasn't until we read in the newspaper that London had
denied all knowledge of this that we became interested.
This was a good omen, because when leading politicians
deny something, it is fairly certain that it is in fact taking
place. Hard on the heels of this denial came another
official handout, hinting that certain conditions must be
met before any talks could be contemplated. The first
prerequisite was unconditional surrender: the Irish
Republican Army would have to lay down its arms. From
then on, the political double-talk went from the sublime

to the ridiculous. Asked in the House of Commons if he was prepared to grant safe conduct to representatives of Dáil Éireann, knowing them to be on the wanted list, Lloyd George intimated that, if such persons came to England, they would be subject to the law of the land. This didn't leave the people involved with much choice, since everyone who was anyone in the republican movement was already on the wanted list.

All this, of course, was the usual beating about the bush. From a military standpoint, there was no need for any hurry on Britain's part to end the conflict; its side effects were her greatest problem. She had long since lost the propaganda war: her credibility, both at home and abroad, was being subjected to very critical analysis. She knew she would have to talk to someone sometime, but not before she had signed and sealed an agreement with the hard men of the North, the Ulster unionists. This was to ensure that, in the event of talks taking place, at least six counties of Ulster would be non-negotiable. So it was in an atmosphere of deep distrust on both sides that the talks eventually got under way and an uneasy truce was declared. It is worth noting also that, for all the belligerent questions and answers in the House of Commons about what would happen to wanted men should they set foot in England, the Irish delegation included two men who were specially released from prison to take part in the talks, while the delegation was led by one of the most wanted men in Ireland: Michael Collins.

8
—

ERIN'S PRIDE – AND A NEW POLICE FORCE

At home, politics and talks about talks were now taking second place to a far more interesting happening right on our doorstep. Pat the Tailor, a neighbour of ours, had acquired a racehorse. It wasn't a racehorse really but it looked like one and behaved like one, which was fair enough. In fact I think it belonged to the hunter class, and there was much speculation as to how Pat became the owner of this noble beast. The story that gained most currency was that a departing British officer had had some unpaid bills and had left the horse in lieu of payment. Anyway, the horse was duly registered under the grand and patriotic title 'Erin's Pride', wee Johnnie Black (Pat's next-door neighbour) was appointed jockey and a serious training programme got under way. It was not just with envy but with downright jealousy that I used to watch Johnnie put the Pride through its paces. The pair of them – Johnnie with his cap back to front and lying well forward on the Pride's mane – would tear along on the grass verge, kicking up great lumps of moss as they went.

However, like most horses, the Pride was nobody's

fool; it wasn't long before he had everyone in the neighbourhood in the 'heel of his hoof', so to speak. Those were the days when everyone had time for a chat and would stop to pass the time of day. The Pride soon cottoned on to this local custom, and as soon as he saw someone approaching he would reduce the pace to a trot, until Johnnie stopped for a chat. Then the Pride would be patted and stroked and told he was 'a great baste altogether', but he would just nibble a blade of grass or a leaf from a hawthorn bush and pretend he wasn't interested in all this praise at all. Actually he was enjoying every minute of it. Aside from tough training, diet was the next essential part of the programme. It was considered that at least a dozen raw eggs a day were necessary to keep a racehorse in top form. It happened, however, to be one of those years when, for one reason or another, the hens weren't being too generous and eggs were scarce. So Pat the Tailor had his work cut out going round the houses, collecting an egg here and an egg there, just to keep the Pride in the style to which racehorses are accustomed. Now my father, may he rest in peace, was always a great one for a raw egg himself – two if he could get them – beaten up in hot milk for his breakfast. I can recall as if it were yesterday one of my sisters warning him to 'Go aisey on the eggs; they're scarce.'

'Surely, if Erin's Pride can have a dozen a day, I'm entitled to wan,' he replied.

Soon, however, we were back in the throes of political debate yet again, as the London talks dragged on and on. It was now obvious that our negotiators were having a tough time; the newspapers were forecasting deadlock and breakdown. One bone of contention was the partition of the country, particularly when our men realised that they were being presented with a fait accompli. A treaty had already been drawn up and was awaiting the findings of a mysterious body called the Boundary Commission. This body was already at work amending the map of Ireland. Tucked away up in the north-west corner of the land, the people of County Donegal felt very isolated and insecure. They, more than most, were deeply concerned as to where the line of demarcation would be drawn. The amended map not only showed where the border would be but also made abundantly clear the political and sectarian motives behind Partition. Three counties with mainly Catholic populations – Cavan, Donegal and Monaghan – were lopped off from the old province of Ulster, leaving six counties – Antrim, Armagh, Derry, Down, Fermanagh and Tyrone – with mainly Protestant populations, thus securing an in-built unionist majority which would prevail for all time. Not only did the six counties become a statelet within a state, its status made it unique within any concept of democracy, because it now had dual representation by its own government (later to be sited in Stormont) and elected representatives to the British Parliament at Westminster.

Britain had now secured a permanent bridgehead in Ireland, so all that was left for the men of Dáil Éireann to address themselves to was the remaining twenty-six counties. For these, Britain had presented a package deal in the form of a treaty on a take-it-or-leave-it basis. The twenty-six counties could now have Dominion status and would henceforth be known as the Irish Free State. Britain would retain responsibility for Ireland's external affairs, while the British navy would have access to all Irish ports. In return, the Free State could raise its own army and police force and be responsible for health and education. But, as always, the sting was in the tail. In order to qualify for the new status on offer, the Irish Free State would have to declare an oath of allegiance to the British Crown. This was the setting for the great debate on the proposed treaty that took place in the Dáil and lasted almost a week. Then, after much acrimony and soul-searching, under the slogan 'Freedom to Obtain Freedom', the Treaty was accepted by a majority of thirteen votes. Britain's trump card, the 'split', swept the board. Ireland was torn asunder by a civil war between pro- and anti-Treaty forces which lasted until 1924. During this bitter conflict, the Free State government, in its first year of office, executed more of its countrymen than the British had during the whole of the insurgency campaign. By then the seed for future conflict was well and truly sown, and now, over half a century later, and with tragic consequences, the people of Northern Ireland are reaping the whirlwind.

It was to mark, rather than celebrate, the signing of the Treaty that a public holiday was declared. The big event at home was to be a race meeting, which surprised everyone, since there was no racecourse in Inishowen. There were, however, three fairly level fields running parallel on the outskirts of Buncrana. All that was needed to convert the fields into a temporary racecourse was to cut a few gaps in the hedges. But the whole idea of a race meeting soon caught the imagination of the local inhabitants when it became known that the Pride himself, no less, would be carrying the colours of his owner, Pat the Tailor. So, when the great day dawned, everyone for miles around converged on our temporary course. As well as bookies, there were tinkers, crown-and-anchor men, three-card-trick men and lots of other conmen, all shouting the odds. Refreshments of all kinds dear to the hearts of youngsters were available in a big tent: sweets, buns, cakes of all sorts, the lot. And in a corner of the field in another tent one of the enterprising locals had set up a shebeen and was soon doing a roaring trade in 'wee-still'. As the day wore on, the wee-still began to take effect: those not accustomed to its potency were soon staggering about or lying flat on the grass. Fierce arguments about politics in general, and the Treaty in particular, were soon in full swing.

The republican police had now assumed the role of law-and-order enforcement, and the race meeting was the first occasion we had seen them on duty. What a difficult undertaking it must have been, trying to be a policeman when you didn't even have a uniform to prove that you were one. All the new policemen had to show for their authority were their Sunday suits and armbands. Big Phil, the local Volunteer commander, was in charge. Poor Phil must have had his work cut out, trying to be all things to all men, especially since all the would-be lawbreakers were his neighbours. Somehow he managed, but not without some entertaining moments. The area near the finishing post was cordoned off by a few lengths of stout rope, to keep the public at a safe distance. Our new policemen were taking their crowd-control duties very seriously indeed. There were sharp orders to the crowd to 'Stand back there! Don't lean on the ropes!' Sometimes their orders would be emphasised with 'Git aff the bliddy ropes!'

It was during this exercise that a local character called Wee Dinny came into his own. Dinny was a man of very short stature and used to try to overcome the problem by wearing a long jacket. This innovation tended to make matters worse, because the jacket always seemed to flap round the back of his knees. But when Dinny had a couple of glasses taken, he felt seven feet tall and walked with a swagger. He insisted on helping the new police to keep order round the finishing post. Following close on a policeman's heels, he would repeat every order the policeman gave, word for word – all to the great amusement of the crowd, which included a group of old RIC men. Although their public role as policemen was over, they still wore their uniforms, but they were just spectators like everyone else, so they could afford to have a laugh at the expense of the new lawmen, as well as at the antics of Wee Dinny. But they were told sharply to 'Stanback and git aff the bliddy ropes!' like everyone else. Dinny, however, had reserved a few chastening remarks of his own for them. Bareheaded and rocking back and forth on his heels, he intervened with: 'Git aff the bliddy ropes when the man tells ye!' Wagging a forefinger at the group of ex-policemen, in a loud voice Dinny proudly proclaimed: 'Wes is youse now. So youse can be wes for a bliddy change.' He may have got his pronouns mixed up a little but in his own inimitable way Dinny was expressing the spirit of the times.

As the time for the last race drew near, the spectators began to crowd round the finishing post. It was now that the moment of truth had arrived for Erin's Pride. There were only three entries in the race, so he had only two to beat, and the betting was fairly heavy. Some people were hoping to get reimbursed for all those eggs they had gone without so that the Pride could have a proper diet. With the approach of pounding hooves, the crowd, anxious to get a good look, ignored orders from the police (and Dinny!) about leaning on the ropes. Two horses thundered past almost neck and neck, with the Pride, alas, bringing up the rear at about two lengths. Many tried to put a bold face on their disappointment at the Pride's lack of staying power. 'Aw well! Maybe he just didn't have it in him,' was the general opinion expressed.

Old Mary Begley, who was a staunch supporter of the Pride during his training days, took his failure to heart more than most, She just couldn't resist the temptation to crawl under the ropes and give the Pride the benefit of her tongue. Shaking her fist in his face, she declared: 'Well, bad scran tae ye, ye oul divil ye. If I had knowed ye was going to do the dirty on us, never a wan of my best eggs would iver went down yer gizzard.' The poor old Pride looked really shattered, standing there with the steam rising from him. He was snorting and blowing, trying to get rid of the big flecks of froth which hung round his nostrils. He kept rolling the whites of his eyes at Mary, as if to say: 'Aw, leave orf, missus, I was in the first three, wasn't I?'

The Pride's failure to make the grade wasn't the only source of disappointment for many that day. The over-indulgence of a few men at the shebeen resulted in some fierce arguments, which ended up in one or two fights.

The sorely tried patience of Big Phil and his men eventually gave way; they had no option but to stop all sales of liquor on the racecourse for the rest of the day. This task was carried out in a most unceremonious manner: they raided the 'shebeen' and confiscated every drop of whiskey they could find. Jars and bottles were carried to the edge of the field and the contents emptied into the ditch, amid plenty of disparaging remarks from the onlookers: 'Christ, it's a wicked shame, wasting good whiskey like that,' they said. The shebeen owner wasn't too happy about Big Phil's methods of law enforcement either. 'Well, bad luck tae ye. I'm damned but yet jist as big a hoor as any of them ould black bastards [the RIC] iver was,' he shouted. So, from a law-and-order viewpoint, it seemed that the pigeons were coming home to roost far sooner than many people expected.

9
—

THE 'RABBLES'

The year 1922 was a significant one not only for the nation but for me as well. During the transitional period when the Free State government was assuming its responsibilities, schools were closed for a short period. When they reopened I considered myself too big to go back. I was rising thirteen. The underlying notion those days was that, if a boy thinks he's too big to go to school, then he must be big enough to earn his own living. Later that year, my eldest brother, James, returned from America with the intention of settling down in Sarida. Although we had been a big family, it was surprising how quickly it thinned in the end. As mentioned earlier, my two eldest sisters were already married. The third-eldest, the cheeky one who had the sauce to bandy words with those dangerous men, the Auxies, died later aged twenty-seven. My youngest sister emigrated to America. I had another sister whom, sadly, I never knew: she died in her childhood before my time. That left my brother Charley, who was working somewhere in Scotland and who by the very nature of things would eventually settle down in the Rock.

For yer man then, the writing was on the wall and the message was: 'Paddy, my ould son, 'tis time you were moving out.' So it was that my first steps on the road to fame and fortune led me to the hiring fair in Derry, accompanied by my father. The hiring fairs, or 'rabbles', as they were called, were held twice a year in May and November and lasted three weeks each. The period of contract was six months. If the twelfth of May or November happened to fall on a Wednesday, that was release day. If the twelfth happened to fall on a Thursday, as it often did, release day didn't occur until the following Wednesday, so the farmer had a free week. The first rabble then was release day, when all the wee boys and girls who had been hired would come home and spend a week with their families. The following Wednesday would be the hiring fair proper, when farmers would be looking for new servants, and wee boys and girls for new places. The third rabble would take place the following Wednesday but it was never popular. Only those farmers who had failed to get someone suitable the previous Wednesday, and boys and girls who had failed to get a suitable place, would attend.

It was the first time I had been to Derry and I found the place a bit bewildering. Everyone seemed to be in a great hurry. The place where the hiring took place was at the top of the Bogside in an area called the Diamond. There was a big crowd there that day, mostly wee boys and girls who, like myself, carried a pathetic little bundle under their arms, which was just a change of washing.

Strange farmers were looking us over. Soon a prosperous-looking gentleman approached and, addressing my father, inquired: 'What are ye esking for the wee boy?'

'Six pounds,' my father replied.

'He's a bit wee. How old is he? Can he milk? Is he any good with horses?' the man wanted to know.

At last a bargain was struck for five pounds ten shillings. The stranger took my bundle, gave me a shilling and told me to meet him back on the Diamond at four o'clock sharp. Then he and my father went off to the nearest 'snug' to clinch the deal over a bottle of stout. Taking the little bundle from you, once the bargain had been struck, was a cute move by the farmer because, as long as you were in possession of it, this was an indication that you were still not hired. So, by taking it from you, the farmer was guarding against anyone else making you a better offer. Also it was a kind of assurance that you would turn up at the appointed place later.

I went looking at shop windows; I'd never seen so many shops before. I found an eating-house and had a great blow-out, and still had thruppence change from my first employer's shilling. I wandered down to the quayside and watched boats being unloaded. Derry was a busy seaport in those days. I was fascinated by the dray horses as they took their heavy loads up the steep incline at the trot, their drivers having to run to keep up with them. Back in the Diamond I met my father again; we both agreed there was no point in him hanging around any longer. The tears weren't far from the surface on either of us as we said our brief farewells – particularly me, as I watched him disappear down the Bogside to catch the train home. But I was a big man now. I was hired. Promptly at four o'clock my boss returned and took me down a street to where a horse and trap were waiting and being loaded with groceries. There was a lady present but she didn't speak. When all the groceries were loaded, I was told to get in the back. It was now almost dark, the streetlamps were coming alive and it was very cold, as we set off at a brisk trot southwards. It had been a long day and I was beginning to feel tired and miserable, knowing that each clip-clop of the horse's hooves was taking me a little bit farther away from home.

In the end I must have dropped off to sleep, only waking up when the trap stopped in a dark farmyard. The place was near Donemana, County Tyrone. I had a meal all alone in the kitchen. Later I was given a lighted candle and told it was time for bed because I had to be up early in the morning. My sleeping quarters were in a loft above the kitchen, and by the smell of the place I concluded it was used for storing seeds as well. The mice squeaked as they scampered for safety when I entered. But I was too tired to worry about small details like that, so I didn't stay awake long. But all too soon, as I recall, I was woken up by a loud banging on the ceiling below and a female voice telling me it was time to get up. It was six o'clock in the morning and pitch dark outside. The lady who hadn't spoken to me in Derry the day before was waiting for me. She had found her voice now all right. With a hurricane lamp already lit and waiting, she was going to show me all the jobs required to be done every day before breakfast. She warned me to pay attention because she didn't have time to keep showing me; tomorrow and thereafter I would be expected to manage on my own.

She showed me where all the animals were, where their

food was kept and also how much to give them. This done, the next job was to muck out a big byre: this job took most of the time. The lady returned with a consignment of buckets, pans and pails and set to milking. I was amazed at the speed with which she carried out this operation: none of your one-handed methods here. By now I had noticed that there were two other men in the yard but in the darkness they were just shadows fleeting in and out of stable doors. At eight o'clock, breakfast time, the two men whose shadows I had seen earlier turned out to be the ploughman and a general labourer; they lived on the farm somewhere in tied cottages with their families. The breakfast was no banquet: a small basin of porridge, two slices of buttered bread and a mug of weak tea. All the rest of the meals were of the same frugality. Neither of the men had much to say, apart from asking me my name and where I came from. However, I did find out what the strength of the household was: a mother, one son and two daughters. The son, who was the boss, never appeared on the scene before breakfast but immediately afterwards he was in the yard giving the two men their orders for the day.

Ignoring me altogether, he told the labourer to start me on the 'snedding'. Armed with a vicious-looking little instrument – a reap hook which had been cut and ground to half its normal size – I set off with the labourer to one of the longest fields of turnips I had ever seen. There had been a hard frost. The ground and the turnip tops were frozen solid – and my fingers were too very soon afterwards as I went topping and tailing, two drills at a time. The labourer left me to it after advising me to keep an eye out for the boss, who no doubt would be visiting me later on. Some time later the two men appeared with cartloads of dung that they deposited in a corner of the field, ready for the spring activities. Then the carts were loaded with turnips and taken back to the farmyard. Loads of dung out and loads of turnips in seemed to be the main activity for the following week or two.

Sunday was the day in the week I looked forward to most. Neither of the two men attended on Sundays so I had the kitchen all to myself. But, greatest of all, I had one sausage all to myself for breakfast every Sunday. I have consumed many of those mysteries since then but none with the same flavour as the ones I had on Sunday mornings in the place near Donemana. As far as I was concerned, there was no social activity of any kind. Except for an hour or two when I went to Mass on Sunday mornings, I never left the confines of the farm all the time I was there. On Sunday evenings I always collected my washing from the ploughman's cottage. His wife did my washing but I was never invited inside; the good woman was always waiting at the door for me when she heard me coming. Once I did get far enough inside the door to notice there was no chimney on the inside of the cottage: smoke from the fire just went through a hole in the roof. There was a big family of young children in the cottage.

I had only been at the farm a few weeks when I had a bad stroke of misfortune. Since the men never attended on Sundays, the boss looked after the horses himself. After dark on this particular Sunday evening, he told me to go up to the loft above the stable and throw down some straw. I was to hurry myself: he was going out and wanted his boots cleaned. In the dark I failed to notice that someone had been stretching tethers in the loft. Tethers were an essential component of farm equipment in those days for securing loads of hay or straw to carts. They were lengths of hemp rope but were cumbersome to use unless they had gone through the stretching process. This was done by soaking the rope in water and suspending it by heavy weights across the rafters of the barn. I didn't see the fifty-six-pound weight suspended above the trapdoor until colliding with it head-on. I fell backwards through the trapdoor down to the stable below. One foot must have got wedged in the bottom rungs of the ladder but the pain was so intense I couldn't tell whether it was my foot or leg that had been damaged. Fortunately, the horses didn't panic; otherwise I might have been trampled on as well. The boss wasn't very sympathetic. 'That'll larn ye to look where yer going,' was his only comment. I hobbled back to the kitchen.

The old lady said my foot was probably only sprained. She gave me a piece of rag and told me to soak it in cold water and tie it round the damaged foot. I got no sleep that night. In the morning the foot was so swollen I went through much agony trying to get my boot on. So I hobbled around mostly on one foot, leaning against the walls where possible. Somehow I got all my jobs done. The men said the foot would mend in a day or two. But it didn't, not in a week or two, or a month or two, or even a year or two. But time is a great healer: the foot got better eventually. Meanwhile, the work had to be done: there was no one excused duties. The dung-out-and-turnips-in routine was now interspersed with 'shough' [ditch]-clearing and hedge-cutting. This was a welcome change: when there was no one about I could hunker down in the ditch and rest my poor old foot.

The next major event on the farm was threshing and, from the comments of the two men, they weren't looking forward to the occasion at all. I discovered why later. The two horses were yoked to the mill and they were so keen for exercise that they went round the circuit almost at the trot. One of the men, with a pitchfork, kept me supplied with sheaves, while I cut the straps and laid the sheaves on the feed-board at the boss's elbow as he fed the mill. The other man worked the front of the mill, clearing the straw away. I was so keen to keep the boss well supplied with sheaves that I soon had a pile waiting for him. That was when he started shouting. But with the noise of the mill, I never suspected that the shouting was all for my benefit, until he picked up a sheaf and hit me over the head with it. He kept shaking his fist at me but I still didn't get the message, until I saw the man with the pitchfork holding up one finger, indicating that the boss wanted only one sheaf at a time on the feed-board.

This arrangement made life much more difficult for me. In the semi-darkness the sheaves got tangled up, my broken foot was very painful and it was hard work trying to keep things running smoothly. The threshing lasted two days and we were all glad when it was over. Apparently, on a previous occasion a piece of binder twine had found its way into the mill and brought the threshing to a halt. No doubt there was method in the boss's madness but he would have made life much easier by simply explaining beforehand how the job was required to be done, rather than after it had been done wrongly. But the boss wasn't the kind of man who confided in servants.

I sometimes thought I was the only one out of step, until one day I heard a battle of words going on between the boss and the ploughman. I was doing a bit of hedging when the ploughman came along with his team and started ploughing in a large stubble field. He had done only a couple of furrows when the boss appeared and the ploughing stopped. Soon the pair of them were shouting at each other. I heard the boss shout: 'Shut up and listen!' Later I watched him stride away across the field, looking very cross indeed. I never asked what the row was about: most probably, in ploughing parlance the field was being scattered instead of gathered, or vice versa. But there was some consolation in knowing that I wasn't the only one who displeased the boss at times. By now I had developed quite a limp but, since I was managing to do all my work, nobody was concerned. Sometimes on a Sunday morning while I was having breakfast, one of the boss's sisters, who was terribly ill with the dreaded TB, would come and enquire about my foot. She was a kindly soul and would have helped if she could.

My last confrontation with the boss took place one spring day when he was sowing corn. The machine used for sowing was known as a 'fiddle': the seed was poured into a small bag attached to the 'fiddle', which in turn was looped round the boss's neck. The seed trickled through the bottom of the bag onto a small metal fan, which had a leather thong with a handle attached. The rotations of the fan and the steps of the sower had to be synchronised, to maintain an even cast. My job was to keep the boss supplied with seed from sacks placed at intervals in the field. Since the little canvas bag held only a bucketful at a time, I had my work cut out trying to keep up with the sower. The ploughman and his team kept close up with the harrows, so any delay on my part resulted in much verbal abuse.

The only thing that kept me going was the knowledge that the May rabbles were only a week or two away. But I had one more surprise to come, and it was a pleasant one for a change. We were having dinner one day when the ploughman remarked to the other man: 'Paddy and I are going for a drive this afternoon.' It was the first I had heard of it, so I didn't ask any questions, lest it be some kind of leg-pull. But promptly after dinner the ploughman and I set off in the trap. I never asked where we were going, because it was such a pleasant surprise to get away from the farm: why look a gift horse in the mouth? After a journey of some three miles, we reined into a small farmyard. A woman was sitting outside her kitchen door, cutting seed potatoes in the spring sunshine. After the ploughman had introduced us, the woman got another chair from the kitchen and invited me to sit down and show her my sore foot. 'It's a poor, poor foot,' she remarked, and I couldn't have agreed more. At a guess, I would say the woman was in her early thirties; she was wearing a sack apron, heavy lace-up boots and a shawl. But, in spite of her workaday clothes, I couldn't help feeling that somehow she was a remarkable person.

Turning her head away from me, she whispered an incantation of some kind to herself; it was inaudible to me. Then she removed a silver ring from her finger – it was so big, it was more of a band than a ring – and moved it gently over the arch of my broken foot. This done, she wished me good luck and said she hoped the foot would soon get better. The ploughman, who had been waiting some distance away, came forward and gave the good woman two half-crowns. Then we set off on our return journey. The visit wasn't mentioned again; it was a fine afternoon and the May 'rabbles' were only a week away. There was no overnight miracle as far as my foot was concerned. But in all fairness, I have to say that night I had the first complete night's rest since the accident happened. On the eve of the May 'rabble' the old lady, who still acted as head of the household, paid me my six months' wages: five pounds in notes and ten shillings in silver. She told me to go and pay the ploughman's wife for my six months' washing: the good woman charged me five shillings. Two carts had been loaded overnight with sacks of corn, so early the next morning the ploughman and I set off with the two carts for Derry. We stopped at a large corn merchant's premises near the quayside. I said goodbye to the ploughman, he wished me good luck, and so ended the saga of the place near Donemana.

10

ISKAHEEN

Derry was crowded with youngsters, all very happy to be on their way home – for at least a week, anyway. The main greeting for the day was: 'Are ye staying on?' It was a kind of slogan for the day; even grown-ups greeted each other in this way as a kind of joke. I even heard an old farmer being asked if he was 'staying on'. 'I doan know if thon oul woman of mine will stan' the sight of me for another six months,' he replied.

Everyone at home was pleased to see me. They all wanted to know why I was limping. I told them I had sprained my ankle. But the week soon went by and on the Wednesday I was back on the Diamond once again, trying my luck for the second time. The May 'rabbles' were always the busiest; many farmers had hired help only in the summer period. Most of this help came from Inish-owen, where both boys and girls had a reputation for being good workers and were much sought after. Apart from wages, places (as the farms were called) were known as good or bad according to whether or not the 'mate' [food] was good. But in all my years at the game I came across only one place that could be classified as good.

It was often said that a farmer could keep a servant for six months and pay the wages and still be in pocket by fattening an extra pig. I remember hearing two stories which represented the extremes, in the good or bad 'mate' situation. One wee boy discovered that the man who had hired him wasn't a farmer at all. He was a retired official of some kind who had a smallholding, one or two cows and a pony. This man and his wife were apparently people who believed in looking after the inner man, and they fed their workers well. Further, they observed a custom that was unknown in farming circles: the mid-morning break. So, for the first time in his life, the wee boy was allowed to help himself to bread and butter. Soon he wrote home, telling his folks about his good fortune, describing it thus: 'I get two breakfasts in the wan morning, and the butter in a bowl.' At the other end of the scale I heard a neighbour describe how, when he was thinning turnips or weeding potatoes, the farmer would come along at dinner time with a few boiled potatoes and just drop them in the drill beside him. In between these two extremes, of course, there was the average, but for my part – maybe it was just me – I was always hungry.

As soon as my second employer spoke to me, I knew he wasn't an up-the-country man; he sounded local. After asking a few questions, he said: 'You won't be far from home if you come with me.' I told him I wanted six pounds. 'That's all right!' he replied. He had a few messages to get, so would I come along and keep an eye on his horse and cart while he did his shopping, he asked. When he was ready, we set off down the Derry–Moville road alongside Lough Foyle until we turned off at a place called Iskaheen. The farm didn't look very big but I discovered later he was a potato man and rented a lot of land. It was still only early afternoon when we arrived at the farm; after a meal, the boss suggested there was still time for a couple of hours' turf-cutting. It was a stiff climb to the moss on top of the hill. Normally turf-cutting is a three-man job, requiring a cutter, a holer and a capper. But since there was no capper I had to do both jobs. I also had to keep an eye on my new boss, who was very enthusiastic with the turf-spade. I didn't want any more accidents, since I already knew one or two men who had lost a fingertip while holding turf. There was a grand view of Lough Foyle from the top of the hill, with boats of all sizes leaving Derry on the night runs to England and Scotland. The boss told me that most of the sheep I could see around were his; this meant there would be plenty of clipping and dipping to do later on. The sun had almost set by the time we got back to the farm. I didn't need any rocking to sleep that night. My sleeping quarters – a loft where all the lumber was stored – were every bit as dingy as those at Donemana. It was a big family: four little girls and, from my brief observation, another one on the way.

Soon I had spoken to most of the neighbours. They were inquisitive and friendly, wanting to know my name and where I came from. One or two commented that I would earn my money that summer: the boss had a reputation for being a hard goer. As I recall, he was a bit of a rush-and-tear man: on most jobs he tried to set the pace but couldn't sustain it. His wife was a very pleasant sort of person, with a nice touch of humour that compensated for her husband's rather dour outlook on life. The 'mate', being more varied, had a slight edge on that in the place at Donemana. The good woman made some very tasty puddings, and to this day I'm a wild man for a good pudding. There was no shortage of work about the place. The working day was usually from seven in the morning until eight in the evening. The forepart of the day was mostly spent thinning turnips or hoeing potatoes. In the afternoons, weather permitting, I would be up in the moss 'winning' turf. But I enjoyed the evenings most. Just up the road a grand old gentleman lived alone in a rather dilapidated old cottage. He was a cripple and could only get about with the aid of sticks. He liked company and kept open house. Many of the local young men would gather there in the evening to play cards or tell stories. Sometimes a 'gentleman of the road' would spend the night there. I liked listening to them; they were great storytellers and had a wealth of experience.

When the hay-making season started, I was called upon to use a scythe for the first time; a swath had to be cut round the field to allow the horses to get round with the mower. It was the first time I had used a scythe, and after one or two abortive attempts I gradually got the hang of it. Getting the correct swing was all-important, rather like that old song: 'It don't mean a thing, if you ain't got that swing.' But you had to have a good back as well; anyone who hadn't was well advised to keep away from the scythe. Anyway, the boss said he had seen worse; coming from him, I took it as a bit of a compliment. So we cut hay, turned it, cocked it, carted it and stacked it. We thinned turnips, hoed potatoes, clipped sheep and dipped sheep, and moved turf from footings to rickles.

Then I had the most pleasant job of all, slipping the turf

from the top of the hill down to the road, where they could be collected by cart. I had the younger of the two horses for this job, a steel grey, and a very good-natured animal he was. I used to ride on the back of the 'slipe' on the way down but it was a long haul back to the top again. There was a fine, panoramic view of Lough Foyle; the Derry boats set sail in the evening and I used to try and imagine who would be on them. It was the time of year when many of the young men around home would be heading for the Scotch hay harvest. Once a month the old Derry paddle steamer used to make the journey down to Moville, where the White Star liners on the Liverpool–New York run used to heave to and pick up the emigrants. I used to wonder how many of them would ever see the banks of the Foyle again. Halfway through the summer, the good woman of the house told me I could go home for the weekend if I wanted to. I took her at her word and set off over the hill, down to Crockaheany, through the Illies to Sarida. Sadly, the visit proved to be a bit of an anticlimax: it was nice to see the folks but my poor old foot wasn't standing up to the long walk at all. It seemed that no sooner had I got home than it was time to start back for Iskaheen again.

The most back-breaking task I had to perform that summer was spraying potatoes. The material used for this job was called 'blue-stone' [copper sulphate]: it was in crystal form, rather like washing-soda, and was diluted by adding water. The spray machine was carried on the back. But no matter how I tried, I never found an easy way of doing the job efficiently. When full, the knapsack container was just about as much as a wee boy could carry. As I moved, the 'blue-stone' splashed about and leaked, and in no time the clothes on my back were soaked. Then the fine spray from the nozzle of the machine blew about, soaking the other half of my body. I could taste copper sulphate for days after the spraying was finished; there was no consolation in knowing that in two weeks' time the whole operation would have to be repeated. By then, of course, I was getting quite accustomed to working in wet clothes; when the weather wasn't fit for anything else, I would be out on the grazing land scything thistles and benweeds. Getting wet through perhaps twice a day and letting the clothes dry on my back was a frequent occurrence. Yet I must have survived, because I can't recall any serious after-effects.

It was a bad, wet harvest that year, and we struggled to secure the corn and potatoes. Nevertheless, the November 'rabbles' came round again once more. Two days before this much-looked-forward-to occasion, the good woman of the house was delivered of a son. But wee boys of my age rarely attached much importance to such matters. In retrospect, however, to a farmer whose family so far had all been daughters, the arrival of a son was something special. The boss celebrated quite a bit for the next day or two and was in good fettle. On the morning when I was about to leave, I went down to the room to say goodbye to the good woman herself. She was sorry to see me go but they didn't keep hired help in the winter. She wished me good luck. I suppose in her youth she had been very good-looking and, in spite of the ravages of time, she was still a handsome person. I liked her very much. The boss took me back to Derry in the cart. He had lots of messages to get and was in a great hurry but as we parted company he said he would keep an eye out for me next May.

11

HIRED AGAIN

The next week soon went by and on the following Wednesday I was back in the Diamond looking for a new place once again. Among the crowd was a very strange-looking character indeed. He had a limp and didn't seem to walk but went around at a kind of jog-trot. He spoke to two or three wee boys but none of them seemed keen to have anything to do with him. Then I noticed he was giving me the once-over but I didn't like the look of him either. I thought the best way to deal with him was to ask for wages he would be sure to refuse. But it doesn't do to judge people by their looks: his bent leg, the limp and the many blue scars on his face could only have resulted from a serious accident. His appearance wasn't improved by a week's growth of beard and a collar yellow with age that looked like it hadn't been washed for a month. His trouser-bottoms and boots were caked in cow-dung and to crown it all he wore his cap with the peak over one ear.

He spoke to me, asking my age, where I came from and where I had been hired before. Then came the crunch question: 'What are ye esking?' 'Seven pound,' says I, not blinking an eyelid. 'I'll gie et ye,' says he, grabbing my bundle. He wanted my solemn promise I would meet him back on the Diamond at four o'clock sharp; it was a long journey and we mustn't miss the train, he said. As soon as he had gone, someone said to me, 'Yer not going with that madman, are ye? Ye shouldn't have given him your bundle.' But I had no intention of changing my mind; a bargain's a bargain and a man is only as good as his word. When I did turn up later in the afternoon, the strange-looking man was waiting for me and seemed very relieved to see me. Besides my bundle, he was also carrying a sack on his back containing groceries, but he wouldn't let me help him by carrying either the sack or the bundle. I was still limping badly myself. As the man with the bent leg kept lurching to one side and me to the other, we must have seemed an odd-looking pair making our way down to the quayside.

In those days a man with a little rowing boat used to ferry passengers across the Foyle to the Waterside. The fare was tuppence a head but it saved the long walk over the bridge. So I found myself leaving the quayside by boat far sooner than I had anticipated, even if it was only a rowing boat. When we reached the platform at the Waterside, there were quite a lot of people waiting; one or two passed remarks about my new boss which made him very cross, so we moved down to the far end of the platform. Hardly a word passed between us throughout the journey. It was dark when we left the train at Limavady Junction. Outside the station, a pony and trap was waiting for us. The boss took the reins and away we went at a steady trot into the dark countryside. The man who met us at the station looked and sounded a youngish man, which indeed he was: he was the number one man on the farm – the ploughman. The boss wanted to know how the young man had got on that day and what he had planned for tomorrow. I wasn't brought into the discussion at all but I gathered that the young man's name was Tommy. Eventually we turned off the main road and up a drive which was flanked on either side by tall fir trees. We stopped at a big house with a big yard surrounded by many outbuildings. The place was near Drumsurn in County Derry.

The boss was a bachelor but by the look of the house inside and the generous meal waiting for us, there must have been a woman about the place sometime. The sleeping accommodation was as usual in the loft, which I shared with the ploughman. But there were one or two refinements which made life a bit more comfortable, compared with the lofts I had experienced so far. There was a lamp and one or two pegs to hang clothes on; this was indeed progress. Sharp at six o'clock next morning the three of us were down in the yard. I was shown all the jobs that from now on were to be my responsibility. Most of the farms those days were of the mixed kind, although some specialised in a particular branch. My new boss was a fat cattleman and the main purpose of my being there was to do the fattening. The fatteners were bullocks; they lived in a large shed that covered one side of the yard. Much is said and written these days about the intensive feeding of animals kept in confined spaces, the argument being as to whether or not this constitutes cruelty. If it does, then conditions were just as cruel in those years.

The conversion rate determines the profit margin;

every pound of food the animal consumed had to be reckoned against the time taken to reach the most profitable market-weight. The main theory behind the fattening game in those days was that if an animal frets, it won't get fat. It will fret if it can't see daylight and not be allowed out to enjoy it; it will also fret if it doesn't get its food at the regular time each day. The building which housed the fatteners was arranged in such a way as to keep them in permanent darkness. They were fed three times a day: at 6 am, 12 noon and 6 pm. The boss was there most days with his watch, making sure there were no hold-ups. Swede, turnips, cotton-cake and lashings of hay and straw was the main diet. The cotton-cake contained a high percentage of linseed oil, and once the smell of the stuff got into your clothes, it was impossible to get rid of it.

In between feeding-times, the work routine was much the same as at Donemana: loads of dung out and loads of turnips in. The neighbouring farm was owned by the boss's brother, who was also a bachelor. He was a very quiet man who lived in the shadow of his elder brother. The two of them used to have some fearful rows at times and wouldn't speak to each other for weeks afterwards. Not only was my boss an odd-looking character, he behaved most oddly at times as well. When he was upset, he would burst into hysterics; the whole neighbourhood could hear him. But nobody took much notice, and once the tantrums were over he forgot all about them. The daily household chores of both farms – milking, cooking, washing and cleaning – were taken care of by the women-folk of a family living nearby. They and their forebears had been employed in this capacity for generations. They were highly respected and their menfolk were all first-class ploughmen.

Ploughmen were a special breed in those days: their status on the farm was sacrosanct, they lived for their horses and they took a great pride in their craft. Only in extreme emergencies would they assist with other animals on the farm. No farmer would be foolish enough to inspect a ploughman's work while he was doing it. I heard of a young farmer – a keen type new to the game – who went along to see how the old ploughman was getting on. As soon as he entered the field, the ploughman stopped his team; resting on the plough-handles, he began to fill his pipe. He just sat there, having a quiet smoke, until the new boy got the message.

My colleague the ploughman used to disappear every night on his bicycle, never returning much before ten pm. He was a regular visitor to some of the neighbouring houses. Later I was invited to the homes of the womenfolk who worked for the boss. This was a sociable gesture which I appreciated very much. They were great hosts. Mostly we played cards but some evenings there would be a bit of a sing-song, which everyone took a turn at. One woman's husband had just returned from America: he was great craic, especially when he had a glass or two taken, and he also had a nice singing voice. Someone was soon asking, 'What about the wee man from Donegal?' I was expecting this with some apprehension, thinking that any old ballads I might know would sound too seditious on that side of the border. But I couldn't have been more wrong: they hadn't heard any of them before and wanted

to hear them all. In the end I had to write them all out
for the Yankee. It was certainly a much more pleasant
winter than the previous one at Donemana.

The boss still had his hysterical outbursts but I hadn't
been the direct cause of any of these so far. I remember one
morning when the good woman who did all the chores was
late arriving. The boss was in the yard shouting his head
off when the good lady pedalled into the yard on her old
bicycle. She dashed into the house, gathered up her milking
utensils and headed for the byre, while the boss still shouted
at her. As she passed him, she shouted back: 'Ach, git outa
my way, ye oul eejit, ye.' At the same time she gave him a
hard push; he overbalanced and fell, and just lay there
screaming at her. Then he got up, dusted himself down and
disappeared into the house, and that was the end of that.

My one and only confrontation with the boss had some
bizarre consequences. It was a Sunday evening. I had
spent the afternoon in a neighbouring house playing
cards, forgetting all about the time until it was past six
o'clock, and feeding-time. I hurried back as fast as my
sore foot would allow, but too late: I could hear the boss
long before I got there. As I entered the yard, he was
carrying a large basket of sliced swedes to the fatteners,
and was now in the hysterical stage. I never knew what
possessed me at the moment. Stood against the wall was
a pitchfork. I grabbed it and, holding it straight in front
of me, I charged towards the boss. Had he stood his
ground, I would have run past him, for I had no intention
of harming the man. But, terror-stricken, he dropped the
basket, ran into the house and bolted the door. He went
upstairs, opened a window and continued to shout at me.

But, knowing I had won the first round, I didn't take any more notice and carried on feeding the fatteners.

Soon all was tranquil again. I wanted my tea, so I tried the kitchen door and found he had unbolted it again. He must have gone to bed, for that was the last I saw of him that day. The neighbours, of course, all heard the shouting and wanted to know what it was all about. When I told them my story, it was great news. They in turn embroidered the details a bit, so for the next week or so the main craic was: 'Did ye hear that the wee fella from Donegal nearly murdered so-and-so with a pitchfork?' The sharpest comment came from the boss's brother when he heard the story. 'Sarves him right! I wonder someone didn't do it years ago,' said he. The final effect of the episode was to enhance my reputation a bit. I was no longer a fella to be trifled with. But as far as the boss and I were concerned, the matter was closed and never mentioned again.

It was now spring and the fatteners were considered have reached slaughter-weight. There were no cattle transporters in those days, so the poor brutes had to make the last journey on the hoof. But first, certain precautions were essential: the animals had to find the use of their legs. Two days before they were due to go and an hour before their evening feed, the yard gates were shut and a layer of straw spread round the yard. Then the fatteners were let loose. This was the first time they had seen real daylight for six months or so: they just went mad. He would be a brave man indeed who would venture among them for the next hour. It was a cunning move, letting them loose just before feeding-time, for the only way to get them penned up again was by offering food, and even then one or two of them still preferred the daylight. The next evening the exercise period was extended to two hours. The following morning they were driven off to Limavady. I was glad, apart from seeing them off the premises, not to be further involved in the operation. I had no desire to accompany these great innocent beasts to their slaughter. Among them were one or two favourites who used to stand close to the rails to have their ears scratched and ask for more with a friendly nudge of their massive heads.

Alas, there was no time for sentimentality about animals. Now they were gone it was time for me and Caesar to start clearing the pens, where by now dung had risen halfway to the roof. Caesar was a Clydesdale of massive proportions in all departments; he had been a stallion and had served as a stud. It didn't take much imagination to picture him in his heyday, the pride of many a fair and marketplace. Indeed, some of his regalia and rosettes still decorated the stable walls. I never knew the true story of his fall from grace. It must have been serious, for he lost not only his licence but a vital section of his 'testimonials' as well, and was finally reduced to the ranks of an ordinary working horse. He always wore a kind of hangdog expression, as if he never forgave the humans who had heaped this indignity on him. And who could blame him? But like myself he had a sweet tooth, so we built up a working relationship based on mutual respect. I knew he could wipe the floor with me anytime he felt like it, but he, with all the cunning of his kind, probably thought: 'I'll let this fella think he's the boss, as long as he looks after me.' Looking after Caesar meant all sorts of dodges, like stealing bits of cake, breadcrusts, apples and sugar lumps. I'm sure the good woman who did the cooking must have wondered where all her sugar lumps were disappearing to. I think she knew but, bless her heart, she never let on. It took a week to clear the pen; then the walls and surroundings were whitewashed, and the wind and the weather completed the job of fumigation, ready for the next lot of inmates in the autumn.

The seeds were now all in the ground, with only one week to go to the May 'rabbles' once again. It was to be a tough week, however, because enough turf for both farms had now to be cut. It was a long walk back and forth to the moss, which was on top of a mountain. Two men from the other farm and myself cut all the turf. Although the principle was the same, the technique used was very different to what I had been used to. One man prepared the 'bink' (bank) by paring away the top sod. The turf-spade was called a 'slane', but instead of using it in the normal vertical digging position, he used it horizontally, pressing forward into the bink. Each turf was loaded onto a barrow specially designed for the purpose: a long wooden frame mounted on a wheel. My job was to move the loaded barrow and empty it at intervals along the top of the 'bink'. It seemed to be an untidier and much more difficult method than the one I knew, but there were compensations. As I mentioned earlier, this was the one place where the 'mate' was good and plentiful, so for the turf-cutting the good woman who did the cooking did us proud indeed: home-made soda bread, boiled eggs and lashings of strong tea. We usually got a nice fire going from last year's turf; dinner times were great. After a good tightener, I would stretch myself on the heather; I thoroughly enjoyed the sound of silence except for the call of a passing snipe or the bleat of a young lamb away in the distance. In spite of the hard work and my aching limbs, somehow it felt good to be alive.

I spent my last evening calling on all the people with whom I had become friends and who had been kind to me. They were nice people; I would miss them. Next morning the boss yoked the piebald pony and trap and drove me back to Limavady Station. We parted good friends. He always hired a wee girl for the summer period but he would be keeping an eye out for me come November. I didn't realise, of course, that in a week's time I would be passing through Drumsurn again. Meanwhile, I was looking forward to a week at home.

12

Kilrea Fair and a Winter at Home

I was getting hardened to the hiring game now and on the following Wednesday, back in the Diamond, I was asking for seven pounds with confidence. The man who seemed to have no quibbles about the amount intrigued me quite a bit, since he spoke with an American accent. Later I discovered the accent had been acquired; he was a returned emigrant, having spent a considerable number of years in the steel mills of Pittsburgh, USA. It soon became evident that he had damaged his health in the process as well. The new place was somewhere in the hinterland of County Derry. When we alighted from the train at Drumsurn, a lady with a horse and trap was waiting for us. She seemed a pleasant enough person and wasn't the man's wife, as I had first thought: she was his niece. We set off on what proved to be a long journey up one side of the mountain and down the other. Eventually we arrived at the new place, which was in the centre of a small community near the town of Garvagh.

Generally speaking, a guide to the size of a farm is the number of outbuildings it has. My first impression was that this farm wasn't very big. It had been a long day and I was tired, so after a meal, and as soon as it got dark, I went to bed. My sleeping quarters were up in the loft as usual. There was no light so, after banging my head on the rafters a time or two, I had to remember to keep my head down. My first job next morning was to collect the cows from a nearby field and bring them in for milking. While my new mistress was doing the milking, I cleaned the stable and did other odd jobs about the yard. Even if she wanted to, the mistress didn't have much time for talking: besides the milking and preparing breakfast, there were two or three children to be got ready for school. She didn't appear to be in a very good temper, though perhaps the pince-nez glasses she wore added to the severity of her countenance.

After breakfast, my new boss yoked a horse and trap and said we were going to cut turf. The journey took us a considerable way back on the road we had come the day before. We stopped at another farm, and loosed the horse and put him in a stable. The boss introduced me to the people who owned the place: three women (a mother and two daughters), the youngest of the trio being the one who had met us at Drumsurn. It turned out that the elderly lady was the boss's sister. The farm was mostly rough grazing, stocking hundreds of sheep, and was known as 'the mountain'. They were waiting for the turf-cutter to arrive, and when he did, one of the daughters and I accompanied him to the moss. I was glad they were using the old technique instead of the barrow; the cutter set a sharp pace to start with. But cutting turf can tire the best of men and this fellow was no exception. I suppose he could be classified as a general labourer who moved around from farm to farm, doing a week here and a week there. But he was a pleasant enough chap and a good worker. I learned later that he was on the run from the army; perhaps that was why he kept on the move.

My work routine settled down to three days a week on the boss's farm and three days at his sister's place. I found the latter the more pleasant. The meals were generous and, since I was always being told I had a lean and hungry look about me, perhaps the women took pity on me. Because of his poor health, a half-day's work was the boss's limit; then he had to rest. His home life wasn't too happy: his wife seemed to resent the time spent on his sister's place, and there was tension and frequent rows. When these broke out, I used to make myself scarce and spent a lot of time with the people next door, who were very friendly. They also had hired help: a very tall man who walked with a stoop and whom everyone called 'Big Jimmy'. He was an ex-soldier and a bit of a loner. He owned a brand-new bicycle, which he used to let me ride round the lanes. So he was my hero.

One job which had to be done every Sunday afternoon, come what may, was sheep-counting. I know now that counting sheep's legs and dividing by four just doesn't work. The boss and I would drive to the mountain, he to have a quiet afternoon's rest while one of the women and I and two collie dogs went off sheep-counting. The collies didn't have to be told what to do; they knew the drill and set off at top speed, one to each side of the moorland, while the woman and I walked for about a half-mile until we reached an old quarry. There we would sit, dangling our legs over the edge, until the dogs appeared, marshalling a large flock of sheep. While the dogs stood guard at the quarry, the woman and I waded in amongst the sheep, counting. I don't think I was much help to her; she was much more experienced than me. As well as counting, she was also keeping an eye out for signs of disease; any doubtful ones got a dab of paint on one of their horns, so that she could keep an eye on them. The main sheep diseases in those days were foot-rot and maggots – each being a very nasty complaint.

But the good woman could handle sheep in the same efficient manner as she did most other jobs on the farm. Stocky, and wide of haunch and shoulder, when it came to clipping she could have a sheep on its back and the clippers going while I was still making up my mind which horn to get hold of. I often wondered why the young men in the locality never seemed interested in her. Either they were a slow lot or they just couldn't compete with her. Had I been twenty years older, I might have been tempted to throw my old cap in the ring. But then she would have been on the wrong side of fifty and I still wouldn't have been a match for her. In contrast, her elder sister hardly ever appeared out of doors. She was tall and thin, and even an unobservant person like myself couldn't help but notice the dark shadows around her wonderful eyes. She suffered from what everyone called 'the decline' – a polite term for the scourge, tuberculosis, which was taking a heavy toll in lives throughout Ireland at the time.

I spent most evenings with the family next door. They were very sociable people and their hired man, who came from Newtoncunningham, was great craic. As well as being a farmer, the next-door boss was also a road-metal contractor for the county council. Perhaps that was why I found him so interesting; he knew all about quarries, dynamite, stone-crushers and the rest. The summer seemed to go by very quickly indeed, as all the routine jobs – turnips, potatoes, hay and turf – were attended to in turn. Just before harvest-time there was an important event which I remember well: the autumn sheep fair at Kilrea. On the previous day all the sheep on the mountain were rounded up; those for sale were penned for the night, ready for the long journey to Kilrea next morning. The road to Kilrea over the mountain was rough. The casual labourer was in attendance for this occasion and he, I and the two collies did the droving while the boss and his niece led the way in the trap. Once we got the sheep away from their home surroundings, they settled down, following the horse and trap. The two collies were in their element. This was the sort of work they lived for: they guarded the flanks, making sure there were no escapees. All the other man and I had to do was walk behind.

Apparently the sheep already had a reputation for coming from good-quality stock. This was evident when we got near Kilrea by the number of farmers and dealers looking them over and picking out the ones they wanted. Once the sheep were penned, the collies' job was finished; they didn't like the noise and activity of the fair, so they climbed into the trap out of harm's way. The casual labourer and I were told that if we went to a certain eating-house at dinnertime and gave the boss's name, we could have all our wants attended to. I don't know what the other man got, but I was given a half-crown spending money – a very nice surprise. The other man soon disappeared and, considering his circumstances, I wasn't surprised. A crowded marketplace isn't the best place for a man on the run: the army has a long memory.

I spent most of the day wandering round the fair, until the sheep were sold and all the shopping done. It was well into the afternoon when we started the long haul home. With four of us plus the two collies, the trap was well loaded. But the horse didn't mind a bit: he too was glad to be on the way home, and I think our ex-soldier friend breathed a sigh of relief as well. The boss, having had one or two half-ones, was in really good fettle for the first time since I had met him. We stopped at his sister's place for a meal, so it was almost dark when we eventually reached the farm. It had been a long, tiring and memorable day, and a very pleasant one until we arrived back. The good lady of the house was in one of her moods. The air was very tense, so I quietly slipped next door.

It was a busy harvest, with much coming and going between the two farms. We could have used extra help but there was none available. However, all was secured by the time the November rabbles came round again. The boss drove me back to Drumsurn and we stopped at his sister's place while I said goodbye to the three women: they were decent people who had been kind to me. Going down one of the hills, my friend whizzed past us on his bicycle. 'See you later,' she shouted as he sped past. The boss left me at the station and wished me good luck, saying he hoped he would see me again. I liked the man and felt a considerable amount of sympathy for him. He was under a certain amount of domestic pressure and this, together with his poor state of health, meant that he wasn't getting much pleasure out of life.

Derry was crowded, as was usual on rabble days. 'Are ye staying on?' could be heard everywhere. I was wandering down a side street, going nowhere in particular, when I spotted my old friend from Newtoncunningham. Bareheaded, he was leaning against the wall of a public house; had it not been for the wall, he would have been lying on the ground. It wasn't yet dinnertime and already he was drunk and incapable. I felt so sad for him: he looked so lonely. Yet I knew he would never want me to see him in such a condition, so I crossed over to the other side of the street. I had already made up my mind to spend the coming winter at home. I had been away for two years and felt the need to catch up with local events.

Winter was always the best time to be at home; all the young men would have returned from their summer wanderings in Scotland once the harvest was finished. One could always be sure of a 'big night' somewhere, particularly on Sunday nights. We would probably attend two such gatherings in the course of the evening and then finish up in the Illies dance hall, where dancing continued until two or three in the morning. During the week, most nights were devoted to card-playing. We would foregather in anyone's house and were always welcome. Some nights, weather permitting, we would gather in a place called 'Daniel's Lane', chatting until bedtime. Many a good night's craic took place in the lane, as we sat in the shelter of a high ditch; although the wind whistled through the whin-bushes on top, it was as cosy as being indoors. The subjects discussed were far-ranging, like experiences of times good and bad at the Scotch harvest, rumours about weddings or where the next big night was going to be held – and, of course, women. It was always interesting to hear which young lady was considered to be the best 'hoult' of the year. This discussion always left me very eager to find out for myself just what it all meant. Just what sort of credentials did a girl have to have to qualify for this dubious honour?

13

ON THE ROCKS

My intention was to stop at home until the May rabbles in the spring, but I changed my plans on receiving a letter from Garvagh. It was from the road-contractor's family, written by the good lady of the house herself. It was now early February and I was offered three pounds to come and give them a hand until the rabbles. If I agreed to the offer, my fare would be paid to Drumsurn, where I would be met. Being surplus to requirements at home, I accepted. My new boss met me at Drumsurn, as agreed. He was a very pleasant sort of man indeed, and easy to get on with. Although he had a fairly large farm, he wasn't really a keen farmer; his main interest was in his road-metal contracts. This was a kind of paradox in a way, because he suffered badly at times from a chest complaint, and working in quarries and being exposed to stone-dust didn't help much. However, my new boss preferred the quarries to the fields.

Three people, be it three men or two men and a boy, were the absolute minimum required for quarry work. Holes had to be drilled in the rock face with hammers and a jumper, with two swinging the hammers in alternate strikes while one turned the drill. Swinging a fourteen-pound hammer can be a tiring exercise, so it was nice when my turn came to sit down and turn the jumper. But since it had to be turned after each strike, there was no time for daydreaming. When sufficient holes had been drilled to the required depth, they were charged with dynamite. The boss took the responsibility for this touchy operation. When everything was ready, I had the job of taking up a position on the road nearby, equipped with a red flag. Although the only approaching traffic might have been just a horse and cart a mile away, nevertheless I was fulfilling the regulations to the letter. I felt most important with my red flag, ready to warn the public that blasting operations were in progress.

Once the fuses were set alight, it wasn't long before a series of dull explosions rent the quietness of the hillside. As a cloud of yellow dust rose skywards, every crow in the neighbourhood complained bitterly about the disturbance. The next task was to tackle the shattered rock face with crowbars and sledgehammers; the broken rock was then stacked, ready for the crusher later in the year. For all the hard work, the quarry had its compensations. When the mist and rain closed in, which was often, we would move to a nearby house, where there was always a warm welcome for us. Soon tea would be on the go, but better still from the men's point of view, a wee drop of the hard stuff; not too much – just a couple of half-ones to warm them up. Then our host would call on the boss for a song. He was a fine singer, with a repertoire of songs, none of which I had heard before. But he handled them so well I can still remember the titles of some of them, such as 'The Rose of Aranmore', 'The Boys of Coleraine' and 'The Glen of Aherlow'. After a while, the man of the house would be persuaded to return the compliment, and he was no mean exponent of the art either.

It was because of my boss's low baritone style that I got the title of his favourite song wrong: it sounded like 'The Bonny Shores of Erin' but it was of course 'The Bonny Shoals of Herrin''. Anyone who has ever heard songs by that great Derry singer John McGitten will appreciate my mistake. Of all the boss's songs, 'The Glen of Aherlow' was my favourite. It told the very sad story of a soldier laddie who was blinded on the battlefield at Sebastopol. Discharged from the army on a pension which only lasted a few months, he had to trudge the countryside as a beggar in order to get a living. But the real tragedy was that he would never again be able to see the place he loved so well, the Glen of Aherlow:

My name is Patrick Sheehan;
My years are thirty-four.
Tipperary is my native place,
Not far from Galtymore.
I came from honest parents
But now they're lying low,
And many a pleasant day I spent
In the Glen of Aherlow.

With the advance of spring, the quarry-work had to be abandoned until all sowing was done; this was restricted to just enough for domestic and stock use. The remainder of the farm was devoted to flax, or 'lint', as we called it. Irish linen still played a leading role in the fabrics industry and lint was a good economic proposition for growers.

My three months' contract was nearly finished. A day or two before the May rabbles, I was invited to stay on for the summer period. With the quarry bug fresh in my blood, I accepted. I went home for rabbles week, and for the first time I was able to tell everyone I was 'staying on'. But the week's holiday was soon over, so back to Garvagh I went, to begin my fresh contract. I noticed that in the farm next door, where I had spent the previous summer, the only additional help they had was a local woman on a part-time basis. I met my old boss on numerous occasions and he was always affable, but not so his good lady. I bade her the time of day once or twice but she never acknowledged my salute. I never found out the reason for her odd behaviour.

Apart from the change in work-routine, from field to quarry, this place had an additional attraction: the boss's bicycle. It was no ordinary machine but a road-racer, complete with dropped handlebars, three-speed gears – the lot! Every wee boy's ambition in those days was to get his hands on a bike; it mattered little which breed, providing it had two wheels that went round. I used to wonder just how many venial sins we committed as youngsters by sneaking out from Mass during the sermon for a bike ride. We could take our pick from the many bicycles left leaning against the wall, but ladies' bikes were always our favourites, since there was no crossbar to get in the way. We must have missed head-on collisions by fractions as we whizzed round the chapel, keeping one ear cocked for the end of the sermon. Therefore, to have free access to a posh road-racer any time I wished was a joy forever.

The arrival of the stone-crusher was one of the important events of the summer. A massive piece of machinery this was, drawn and powered by an equally large coal-burning steam engine called a Foden. The two men in charge of the crusher were brothers, and a great pair of characters they were. They had to bring their machine from the other side of the mountain over a rough road, where the possibility of getting bogged down was ever present. They were used, however, to manoeuvring in tight corners, since during the winter months their job was taking their threshing machine around farms. For them, the journey and the setting up of the machine in the quarry was a day's work.

It was essential, of course, that a good head of steam was ready in the Foden every morning, so that operations could start promptly at eight o'clock. It was only natural that I was selected for the job of lighting the fire and, as I recall, I didn't need much coaxing to take on the responsibility. I doubt if many wee boys would turn down the opportunity of having a real steam engine in their sole care for about an hour and a half daily. I didn't need an alarm clock to get me out of bed those mornings; not only was I going to get steam up but I also had the boss's road-racer to get me there. So, with head well down and coat-tails flying, I would pedal up one hill and freewheel down the next. At that time in the morning, the only other living thing on the mountain road besides myself was the odd hare, hopping across from one side of the road to the other. This was a real man's life. When the two brothers arrived, however, they had a good laugh at my expense; no doubt they had seen it all before. I had the Foden ready to start, all right, but in the process I had managed to get myself looking as black as possible with coal dust and grease. Not much point in being an engine-man, I thought, unless you look like one. 'How did ye light 'er, Paddy?' asked one of the brothers, laughing. 'Did ye climb down the reek-stack?'

The older of the brothers mounted the Foden's platform and shifted the throttle-lever. The Foden coughed a time or two as puffs of black smoke rose into the morning air. The great belt to the crusher took the strain, the two shining brass balls on top began to spin and, with earth shaking around us, the crusher took its first mouthful of rock. The large lumps of rock had to be wheeled up to a platform, where the younger of the two brothers had the job of feeding the crusher. I did the wheeling: it was a hard push up a plank set at a steep angle but I was able to run on the way back, since the plank acted as a kind of springboard and there was always another load waiting for me as soon as I put the empty barrow down. Now and again we would change over and I would be allowed to feed the crusher. Sometimes I toyed with the idea of choking this insatiable monster by wedging the biggest rocks I could find between its jaws. I was hoping the belt would come off and we could all have a wee rest until it was put back on again. But this was only tilting at windmills: the Foden just coughed a little louder, a few more red-hot sparks would fly skywards and the crusher would gobble a bit faster, as if to say: 'Aha! Better men than you have tried the oul trick, Paddy boy.'

The crushing lasted a week, and in spite of the hard work, I enjoyed it. The 'mate' was good and plentiful, we did our own brewing-up in the quarry and the fine June weather was at its best. The result of the week's crushing was a large amount of road metal, which had now to be carted to sites along various roads. The sites were specially designed so that the length, depth and width of the metal could be measured accurately by the county surveyor. It so happened that I had to do most of the carting. As I mentioned earlier, the boss suffered from a bad chest, and the dust from the crusher was having its effect. He was confined to bed for a week or two, so I was left to manage as best I could. I felt quite proud, having been allowed to handle a pair of horses. They were good-natured animals and never attempted to take advantage of the 'wee fella'. The younger one was the faster of the pair, so I always kept him at the back, while the older one just plodded on at a nice steady pace. On steep hills I took them up one at a time, leaving the other one to graze until it was his turn. I suppose I must have felt like those old Derry carters in the famous ballad: 'I was free and aisy to jog along.'

I was glad to see the boss back on his feet again, however, because another important task – lint-pulling – was looming. This was very much a community effort: as soon as the lint was ready, the neighbours, without asking, would gather in the field and start pulling. We in turn would go and help them. August was the lint month; there were no mechanical aids in those days, so it had to be done by hand. Not only was lint-pulling a back-breaking operation, a 'knack' had to be acquired as well. You had to gather as much as both hands and forearms would hold and hope that, with a quick jerk of the knee, the lint would come clean out of the ground. Any other way, and you would soon finish up with cut fingers. Sometimes there would be as many as a dozen people in the lint field, women as well as men. Indeed it was already recognised that lint-pulling came much easier to the women than the men: the women were much more supple. But there was always plenty of banter and leg-pulling, which helped to overcome the monotony of the job.

On the evening when the pulling was finished, the party spirit would take over. After a high tea, the evening would be rounded off with a song or two by the local experts. The lint harvest was very much a labour-intensive business. Pulling was only the beginning; next the sheaves had to be carted to a dam and packed in like sardines in a tin. The dam was filled with water, and during fermentation the lint gave off a sickly sour smell which could be noticed a long way off. After two or three weeks it was retrieved and spread on the grass to dry; then it was gathered into sheaves again, stooked and stacked. Finally it was put through the threshing machine; this operation was called 'scutching'. The lint eventually went to market as a fibrous product called 'tow'.

Once again it was harvest time, and the corn and potatoes had to be secured. Any spare time in between was devoted to tidying up the road-metal sites, ready for the county surveyor's inspection. Then the boss would be paid whatever was due to him. It had been a busy summer and I felt that I had earned my seven pounds, but on the whole I'd enjoyed it. On the day of the November rabbles, the boss drove me back to where he had found me at Drumsurn Station. The small boy of the family was a bit misty-eyed when it came to saying goodbye, and the dog, which was a great friend of mine, couldn't understand why he wasn't allowed to accompany me on this occasion. This was to be my last rabbles. I was finished with the hiring game and it was time to move on to something else. I had made up my mind to stop at home that winter, come what may. I had a strange feeling that this would be my last opportunity to do so, and I was right.

14

TRIPLE ALLIANCE

During my absence a new personality had settled in our neighbourhood and was already making a great reputation for himself. He was none other than the sergeant in charge of the first detachment of Civic Guards, who inherited the law-and-order business from the old regime in Buncrana. The sergeant wasn't a tall man by police standards but whatever he may have lacked in inches he made up for in enthusiasm. His main target was the 'wee-still' makers, so it wasn't long before he was nicknamed 'Wee Jimmy' and 'a tarrible man altogether'. Jimmy and his men would make forays, raids and searches, any hour of the day or night, seven days a week. In the end, the mere rumour that Jimmy was planning another raid was sufficient to cause panic among the 'wee-stillers'. They weren't taking any chances, and many a barrel of 'wash', or pot-ale, as we called it, was destroyed on the strength of one of Jimmy's rumours. We had a grand old neighbour who could always be relied upon to supply a drop of 'mountain dew' at any hour of the day or night and at the right price. That was until one peaceful Sunday afternoon when Jimmy and his men burst into her little house. From Jimmy's point of view the raid was a success; he found enough evidence to prove it. Afterwards the old lady was asked what she thought of the new 'polis'. 'Ah well now! That was wan thing about the oul black polis: they never bothered a body on a Sunday,' she replied. Bless her old heart, she recognised that the only thing that had actually changed was the colour of the uniforms.

We had another neighbour who proved to be more than a match for all of Jimmy's cunning. The secret of her success was a big buck-goat which she kept tethered in a field near the main road. The goat was a most treacherous animal indeed; nobody but the lady herself dare go near it. It used to gallop round in a circle on the end of its tether, threatening passers-by by rearing up on its hind legs and dunting the air with its sharp horns. Jimmy and his men were fascinated by the antics of the goat every time they passed. They would get off their bicycles, lean over the ditch and taunt the animal as much as they dared. Having had their fun, they would mount their bikes and pedal off about their business. They were totally unaware that where the goat's tether was staked to the ground the whiskey jar was also buried. Were it in Fort Knox, it couldn't have been more secure.

Father Doherty the parish priest, who for a long time had been waging a lone campaign against the 'wee-stillers', now had a powerful ally in the person of Wee Jimmy. This partnership developed into a kind of triple alliance when later it was joined by another powerful figure, a man called Louis Walsh, the circuit court judge. The law, which had been deemed too lenient for poteen offences, was tightened up. The maximum fine was set at one hundred pounds and the alternative at six months in jail. At that time, the authorities would have had a job to collect one hundred pence, never mind pounds, so the alternative became the norm. But the wee-still makers refused to be intimidated, so it was business as usual for quite a considerable period. Eventually, this punitive measure began to hit some families hard, particularly if it struck during the spring or at harvest time. It meant that wives had to manage as best they could while their husbands languished in Sligo Jail. But, as always in times of trouble, the neighbours rallied round and saw to it that no real harm was done.

There was one interesting case, however, when the roles of husband and wife were reversed. When the husband was due to serve his six-month sentence, he was so ill that the medical authorities deemed he wouldn't survive the rigours of prison. So a compromise was reached – one which I'm sure could never be reached anywhere else except in Ireland. The man's wife volunteered to serve her husband's sentence and the judiciary accepted the offer. Taking the youngest child with her, this stout-hearted lady went off to jail. When she was eventually released, the neighbours agreed they had never seen the woman looking so fit and well before. Nobody gave a second thought to this damning indictment of women's role in society in those times: that a woman, having served a rigorous term of imprisonment, could be looking more fit and bonny than if she been at home doing the domestic chores.

The triple alliance continued to step up its campaign,

with Father Doherty devoting more and more of his sermons to the evils of the poteen trade. Wee Jimmy intensified his raids, while Louis despatched more and more offenders to Sligo Jail. But, if all the stories were true, there were still a few people who would go to any lengths to preserve their immunity from the law. There was old Johnnie Mack, for example, a persistent offender whom Jimmy had brought to book more than once. But Johnnie always had an old hard-luck story ready for his defence: he was a widower; the family had all grown up and left him; who would look after the bit of land and the animals if anything should happen to him; etc. In the past, Louis, after having a word with the priest, who was always in court, had been giving Johnnie the benefit of the doubt. So, with a severe caution or at worst a nominal fine, Johnnie would be cleared, after giving a sincere promise that from then onwards he would mend his ways. The promise wasn't kept, however, and Johnnie soon slipped back into his bad oul ways.

It wasn't long before Jimmy had nabbed him once again. It seemed that on this occasion Johnnie was very worried by the thought that he might have pushed his luck too far. On the day that he was due to appear before Judge Louis yet again, he took a neighbour along, just in case. He went to have a word with the priest as usual, only to receive the shock of his life. 'No, Johnnie,' the priest said to him, 'not this time. Ye let me down. So ye'll jist have to go in there and take yer punishment like a man. Ye'll get no more help from me.'

Poor Johnnie was so badly shaken by this rebuff, he didn't know who to turn to. With his past sins swimming before his eyes, he badly wanted to talk to someone. Well, who should come up the courthouse steps but the local minister for the Church of Ireland, an affable man who always had time to listen to other people's problems? Before he had time to bat an eyelid, Johnnie had him buttonholed and was pouring out his tale of woe. On hearing the story, the minister expressed his regret for Johnnie's predicament but doubted if he could be of much help. It might look a bit odd if he were to intervene, he told Johnnie, adding, 'After all, you're not one of my flock, Johnnie.'

'Ach, true enough, yer Reverence, true enough. But you jist put in a good word for me and I'll soon change all that,' was Johnnie's prompt reply.

In spite of all the risks under the new laws, there were still quite a few wee-still men prepared to take a chance. With these hard men in mind, Father Doherty decided to tighten the screw a little further. He stopped short of excommunication but ruled that absolutions would no longer be available for these offenders at Cockhill. They would have to go all the way to Derry and see the bishop. For a while this new edict didn't seem to be causing too much inconvenience. But as the weeks went by, it became noticeable just how many men were heading for Derry on Saturdays with loads of turf. There was always a good market for turf in Derry; for the regular suppliers, it brought in a few extra shillings and bought a man's baccy. Now the regular turfmen were none too happy about all these johnny-come-latelys to the turf trade: the newcomers were causing a glut on the market. But it was the line of horses and carts waiting outside the bishop's palace on Saturday evenings that began to attract attention.

The story goes that among the group of penitents in the palace waiting room one Saturday evening was a very well-known local character. This man had a great reputation for being an expert on most subjects and was a great talker. So there he was, explaining to his captive audience that by rights he shouldn't be there at all and that someone had made a mistake. But now that he was there, he would do them all a favour by volunteering to be the first man in to see the bishop. 'I won't be long. Sure, me and the bishop are oul friends,' he assured the others as he disappeared into the inner sanctum.

The others sat in silence, no doubt considering what the future had in store for them. Some began to get a bit edgy as the evening wore on and there was still no sign of the bishop's friend reappearing. If each interview was going to take all this time, then it looked as if some of them were going to be there all night. At last the bishop's friend emerged, looking very subdued and crestfallen indeed. The bishop had warned him not to speak to any of the others on his way out but to go on about his business. So, without as much as a wink or a nod to the others, he hurried towards the street door. For a moment there was an air of stunned silence, until another man jumped up and hurried towards the door also. 'Hi! Where are you going? You're the next one in to see the bishop,' someone called after him. The man paused and, scratching his head, said, 'Ach, I don't think I'll bother the bishop the night. If he's got the power on him to put the mockers on thon fella and turn him into a dummy, I think maybe I'll come back some ither time.'

Slowly the combined efforts of the triple alliance began

to bear fruit and the regular 'wee-still' men began to adopt a low profile. They would have a rest for a bit until times got better, so the flow of poteen dropped to a mere trickle. No doubt the big distillery companies, not to mention the Customs and Excise department, were very pleased indeed. They were the people who had been losing money hand over fist to the poteen trade. There was no doubt at all that Wee Jimmy won his spurs in Buncrana and was proclaimed as the greatest 'still-hunter' ever to stride across the pages of its history. He was duly promoted to the rank of inspector and posted away to the south of Ireland where, no doubt, there was fresh territory waiting to be subdued. He was long remembered around Buncrana, where he and his friend, Justice Louis Walsh, carved a niche in local folklore, in the end becoming immortalised in a little balled entitled 'The Cleenka Boys'. This told of an epic battle between Jimmy's men and a bunch of local lads which ended up with bloody noses all round. My brother Charley, may he rest in peace, could always be relied on to give a good rendering of 'The Cleenka Boys' when he was in the right fettle. My nephew Tony Devlin, who now owns the old steading in Sarida, was able to salvage one verse for me, which went as follows:

As I will prove to Louis Walsh,
They say he is the best;
And Sergeant Jimmy Hartigan
By the Pope of Rome was blessed.
But if the Papal blessing be easy got
And bestowed on Imps of Hell,
Then I think that Justice Louis Walsh
Should go to Rome himsel'.

15

The Heysham Boat and Tom Mix

One night during one of our craic sessions in Daniel's Lane, I became very interested in a story told by a young man who had been to the Scotch harvest that summer. Instead of following the usual routine of going to Berwickshire for the corn harvest, he and a friend came south to England. They had heard that a considerable amount of public construction work was going on in Yorkshire and that navvies could always get work. The pay was one shilling and three farthings an hour for a fifty-hour week. Lodgings were available on the job, and by cooking your own food you could save twenty-five shillings a week. To my mind, this was big money and I would have to give it serious consideration. It has to be remembered that in those days there were no further educational facilities available at home; there were no trades or professions to take apprentices, and technical schools were not required. Indeed, the normal requirements of the Education Act were never applied. If you considered yourself big enough to leave school, you did so, and no questions asked. It was against this background that young people would decide to go abroad to find jobs. Since they were unable to compete, either from a trade or educational standpoint, the only jobs available for young men were of the pick-and-shovel kind. Perhaps I was fortunate in this respect. I was always considered to be a big lad for my age: in circumstances where a birth certificate wasn't called for, I could add a couple of years to my age without being questioned. So when I was sixteen I had no qualms at all about going to England to try my hand at navvying.

I arranged to go with a neighbour who was older than me; he had already been to Scotland on two occasions and had some experience. Between us, we gleaned all the information we could from our friend who had been to England the previous summer, so getting some idea as to what navvy life was likely to entail. The first we learned was that a real navvy never spent his money on public transport. If he couldn't cadge a lift, he would walk or tramp. He always travelled as light as possible; a change of washing was plenty but a spare pair of socks was essential. A night's lodging could be had in most large towns for about ninepence in a common lodging house. If you happened to be in between towns once it got dark, it was advisable to get off the road and make for the nearest barn. The police weren't keen on tramps, so they could make life very difficult. Tips of this kind were most useful but my friend and I hoped we would never get into tight corners.

We made up our minds to set off early in February; although our experienced neighbour warned us that it was far too early, we believed that it was the early bird that catches the worm. We started out as we intended to carry on, by walking the sixteen miles to Derry, the nearest seaport. We couldn't have picked a worse day for the journey: it was a cold, raw winter's morning and raining hard. We were soaked to the skin before we even reached Buncrana and our little bundles of washing wrapped in brown paper soon began to look a bit bedraggled. We had got a considerable way along the Derry road when an old lorry pulled up. 'Where are ye's aff to?' the driver asked. 'Derry,' we said. 'Jump in the back,' he told us. We were in Derry much sooner than we had anticipated, and we spent the rest of the day wandering round in our wet clothes; the Heysham boat didn't sail until six in the evening.

The boat that plied between Derry and Heysham twice a week was an old cattle-boat called the *Rose*. The passenger fare for this voyage was eight shillings and sixpence steerage. We went on board as soon as were allowed to do so, mainly to get in the warm. Later we were joined by another young man, who hailed from a place in west Donegal called the Rosses. The three of us were the total number of steerage passengers on the *Rose* that night. The man from the Rosses was on the same mission as ourselves but he had more experience than us. He was going back to where he had worked the previous year and invited us to join him. He told us he knew several of the bosses on the job and felt sure we would have no difficulty in getting a start. We thanked the man for his kind offer but we had made up our minds to stick to our original plan, come what may.

By now the *Rose* was nosing her way slowly down the Foyle and into the gathering darkness. I went on deck to have a last look round but all I could see were a few lonely-looking lights from houses along the Derry–Moville road. I had to admit to myself that the Derry boats which I used to watch and wonder about during my hiring days in Iskaheen were much more romantic than the *Rose* felt just then. As soon as we cleared Moville and began to pick up the swell of the Sea of Moyle, it looked as if we were in for a rough night. Our new friend from the Rosses advised us that the best way to avoid seasickness was to find a suitable place and lie down. Since there were only three of us, at least there was plenty of room; other than that, there weren't many home comforts for steerage passengers on the *Rose*. There was a half-circle wooden bench but the Rosses man warned us we would roll off it once the *Rose* began to show her mettle. We decided the floor was the best place and, after foraging around, we discovered a pile of life jackets stowed away in a corner. We laid these on the floor. The Rosses man went up on deck and came back dragging a large tarpaulin behind him. The three of us stretched out on the life jackets; with a wet tarpaulin for a blanket, we bade each other good-night as the *Rose* took her first nosedive into the Irish Sea.

It was fitful night's sleep, to say the least. At times the *Rose* acted as if she had hind legs and wanted to stand on them. Then she would plunge forward as if to stand on her hand; next she would roll from side to side and give a great shudder, before commencing the next round of manoeuvres all over again. So the night wore on. Although there was a great temptation to get up and move around for warmth, we maintained our prone position.

Eventually, the Rose began to sober up: she was reaching shelter. Soon the noise of the engines faded out and, when the clamour and shouting began above our heads, we knew we had arrived at Heysham. For the life of me I can't think of a more depressing place to be than Heysham Docks at 5 am on a cold, wet morning in February. It was here that we had to say goodbye to our friend from the Rosses. What a nice fella he was! He had to wait for a train to Harrogate, while my friend and I took to the road once again, our next stop Lancaster. It was still raining. We kept hoping that the briefing we had had before we left home wouldn't let us down. We were to look out for a shunting yard near the railway station and carry on to the centre of the town, which was a crossroads. If we took the left fork and proceeded for a hundred yards, we should arrive at the place we were looking for. It was a great relief to find we were spot on target: there the building stood, announcing itself in bold white letters: 'Model Lodging House. Beds for Working Men.'

There was a small cubicle in the hallways and a sign that read 'Ring and Wait'. After a few minutes, the proprietor appeared: he seemed surprised to have customers so early in the morning. We bought three nights' shelter from him for two shillings and threepence each – ninepence a night. Our aim was to be away sharp, first thing Monday morning; we still had a long journey ahead of us. We were allocated beds numbered twenty-nine and thirty, so at least we would be close to each other, but we couldn't help thinking it must be a big bedroom. For the time being, we had no means of finding out: a large notice at the bottom of the stairs read: 'No Admission to

Bedrooms before 7 pm.' There didn't seem to be anyone about the place except ourselves, so we went into a large kitchen-cum-eating room where a large stove known as a hotplate ran half the length of the room. Tables filled the rest of the room, flanked by wooden benches. We were glad to sit down in the warm. We had had no food since leaving Derry.

The proprietor, sensing that we were a couple of greenhorns, told us there was plenty of boiling water in the kettle if we wanted to make tea. He also told us there was a grocer's shop across the street that would supply any groceries we wanted. It was the first time we had had to fend for ourselves in this respect, We decided that, since this was going to be our way of life from here on, we had better make a start. We were hungry. We didn't know that groceries could be obtained in such small quantities as were available in the little shop. But since much of its custom came from the lodging house, it was geared up accordingly. A small packet of tea cost a penny; it was no bigger than a tuppenny Woodbine packet and made two good cups of tea. You could buy twopenn'orth of sugar and a small tin of Nestlé's milk for thruppence. Another thruppence bought a quarter pound of butter, while a large crusty loaf was just fourpence. So we thoroughly enjoyed our first meal in England, although it only amounted to tea, bread and butter.

Later we went for a walk round the town, visiting the railway station to find out about trains. A train journey was part of our itinerary, although it would take us only part of the way to our final destination. We felt a bit foolish on finding out that, for all the tramping we had done that morning in the rain, the fare from Heysham to Lancaster was only thruppence. Clearly we would have to have a close look at the economics of tramping versus trains in future. We were beginning to feel tired after the rough night and the long day; it was almost dark when we got back to the lodging house. The rest of the inmates were returning from their various fields of endeavour. No one took any notice of us as we sat quietly in a corner. We waited for the activity round the hotplate to quieten down a little. Our tea of bread and butter might look a bit mean compared with the big fries of bacon and eggs, sausages and kippers being enjoyed at the table.

Among the crowd round the hotplate, we noticed a man who, at home, would have been an old neighbour of ours. We were quite surprised to see him, since we hadn't heard his name mentioned at home for many years. He was just one of those who had disappeared. From the look of him he was working on a building site. Being old neighbours, we went across and made ourselves known to him, but he didn't seem to be pleased to see us at all. Maybe he thought we were seeking a favour of some kind. Sensing this, we never bothered to speak to the man again, while he ignored us completely. What a sad reflection of the human condition, we thought. But there it was.

We were glad when the sleeping quarters were opened and we could get to bed. Beds twenty-nine and thirty were in the far corner of a very long room which ran the length of the building. The blankets on the narrow iron cots were obviously ex-army; the mattress and pillow were of a rough calico material and filled with straw. But for ninepence a night it was adequate. Three large buckets

were place at strategic intervals down the centre of the
room. I wondered if anyone ever fell over them when the
lights went out. We put our trousers, containing our little
bit of money, under our pillows. We knew the wise thing
to do would be to rest the bed-legs nearest the wall in
our boots. But we were too tired to be overcautious; we
were strangers in a strange land and our main concern
was to get a good night's sleep.

The only disturbance during the night came from the
shunting yard nearby: engines huffed and puffed and
buffers kept crashing away all night. We were the last
ones to get moving in the morning; a quick glance round
the room showed that only two of the thirty beds had
been unoccupied during the night. There wasn't much to
see round Lancaster. We were looking forward to Monday
morning and to being on our way. Whilst wandering round
the town we came across an All-Electric Cinema. We had
heard about cinemas – indeed the subject had been
discussed at length one night in Daniel's Lane. One of the
boys who had worked in Scotland had been to one and
was very excited about this new form of entertainment.
So we decided to go that evening and find out for ourselves; it would pass the time.

A large poster outside depicted a very fierce-looking
man dressed in black, except for a white hat and scarf.
He was astride a fine-looking white horse and had a
blazing gun in each hand. The poster read: 'Now Showing:
Tom Mix in *Tony Runs Wild.*' This conveyed very little to
my friend and me but, erring on the side of economy,
while wanting to have a good look, we got two seats in
the front rows for sixpence apiece. The front rows were

occupied mostly by youngsters, who kept up an incessant din while waiting for the show to begin. Most of them were eating peanuts or oranges and throwing the shells and peel at each other or on the floor. So we had an opportunity of hearing the local dialect at close quarters, and found it very interesting. A great cheer went up when the lights dimmed and shadows flickered on the screen. But this soon changed to whistling and hissing when only advertisements appeared, instead of the crowd's legendary hero, Tom Mix.

Eventually Tom did make an appearance but, not knowing what to expect, it took my friend and me some time to grasp the gist of the story. Most of the action took place in a small town on the American plains. The main attraction of the place seemed to be a large saloon. This was presided over by a big landlady, assisted by two younger women who seemed to spend most of their time hanging around card-players, who occupied most of the tables. Most of the gamblers seemed to be cowboys. Suddenly someone accused somebody of cheating and, in a flash, guns were drawn. But before any shooting started a voice from the doorway ordered everyone: 'Drop your guns!' Then, through the swing-doors, gun at the ready, came the great US marshal himself. Wearing a ten-gallon hat, black shirt and white scarf, very tight trousers and high-heeled boots with spurs a-jingling, he strode across to the bar. The landlady knew him from the old days, away back when he was a gambling man, before he gave it all up to become the toughest lawman in the West. She gave him a great welcome.

There had been a recent epidemic of stagecoach

robberies in the area and much gold had been stolen; Tom was sent to find the villains. He had a suspicion that some of the robbers were among the card-players, and his suspicions were confirmed on going outside and finding that his fine white horse, Tony, had disappeared. Some rogue had unsaddled Tony and chased him into the wilderness, where he had joined up with a herd of wild horses. Tom was very cross about losing Tony, and this dirty trick confirmed his suspicions that the stagecoach robbers were around somewhere. The cinema audience had great sympathy for Tom in his predicament and there were many 'Oh's and 'Ah's from those who felt for him: without Tony, he was badly handicapped. He had to commandeer another horse, of course, to chase the villains, but it was only an ordinary animal – not a patch on Tony. Eventually tracks led him to a rocky escarpment away on the skyline. He knew he was on the right track when shots rang out and went 'ping' as they ricocheted among the rocks. Tom dived for cover but his silly horse just stood there. Tony would have interpreted the situation much more accurately and taken cover also.

The amazing thing about the shoot-out which followed was how the guns kept on firing without being reloaded. That was all except Tom's, which after a while just went 'click'. The audience now began to get very concerned about Tom's future: the villains had him almost surrounded and were creeping closer and closer. The youngsters were shouting: 'Look out, mister, he's coming up behind you!' Indeed, I was beginning to get a bit worried about Tom myself, until I heard one youngster shout to another: 'Aw, shut thy big gob! Tom knows what he's doing.' In spite of his predicament, no doubt everyone was hoping that Tom had a trump card up his sleeve. Away in the middle distance a herd of wild horses were grazing peacefully, the white-coated Tony amongst them. Tom raised two fingers to his mouth and gave two shrill whistles. The audience heaved a great sigh of relief. Tony pricked up his ears and trotted round the herd as if he was giving them instructions. Then the herd, with Tony in the lead, set off in a wild stampede for the escarpment, raising a great cloud of dust, their hoofbeats sounding like a roll of thunder. The villains' horses fled in disorder as Tony led the stampede forward; the villains ran for it as well. Tony, now reunited with his boss, snuffed and slobbered all over him and a great cheer rose from the audience. Then, as Tom, Tony and the relief horse headed for the setting sun, we were invited not to miss next week's stirring episode of Tom Mix and his wonder-horse Tony.

We certainly enjoyed our first sixpenn'orth of the All-Electric Cinema; for a couple of hours, it at least took our minds off our immediate problem. We were in transit, and there would be no peace until we reached our final destination and found whether we would be lucky in finding work. Sunday passed very quickly. The rest of the lodgers seemed to spend most of the day cooking; the hotplate was covered with a variety of saucepans. In lulls in card- or domino-playing there was much stirring and tasting round the hotplate. Everything smelled good, making us feel hungry, but since we had neither the wherewithal nor the know-how, we had to stick to our routine of tea and bread and butter. But we did lash out on a currant loaf, seeing as it was Sunday.

16

THE BARN

We were afoot bright and early Monday morning, with a long day ahead of us. We wanted to cover as much ground as possible during daylight. This stage of the journey was by train to Clitheroe, then on foot across the Yorkshire Moors. We were enjoying the train journey, until I leaned out of the window to view the scenery and my cap blew away. This meant that we would have to spend time in Clitheroe looking for a cap shop, apart from the additional expense of a half-crown, which I could ill afford. Eventually we found a signpost which pointed to Slaidburn, so we hit the road once again. It was then well past midday and soon the weather began to close in on us. The sleet turned to heavy snow and it was bitterly cold. We had no protective clothing, only what we stood up in. Soon we were experiencing blizzard conditions and became anxious about whether we were on the right road or not. The bottoms of our trouser-legs were frozen solid but there was nothing we could do about it except lean against the blizzard and plod on.

We had more or less lost trace of time. It just seemed to be getting dark but gradually it began to clear up a little. We could see the outline of the road and were pleased to find we were still on it. Otherwise it was complete desolation; there was no habitation of any kind as far as we could see, so we pressed on towards the skyline. When we got to the top of a ridge, our flagging spirits cheered up considerably: away in the distance we could make out the straggling outline of houses sticking up out of the snow. This must be Slaidburn. Once there, the back of our journey would be broken, because on the other side lay our destination: a valley deep in the dales of West Yorkshire known as Tosside.

From a distance, this appeared to be a world all of its own. Mountains of freshly dug earth appeared above the snow. Massive cranes seemed to be dotted about everywhere, some working and some with their jibs pointing skywards. Steam engines puffed along narrow-gauge tracks. The whole valley seemed to be alive with all kinds of activity, in spite of the snow. Close to the works area stood the navvies' living quarters: long rows of huts laid out in military style. We had been briefed before we left home that, if we should ever get to Tosside, we should make for the biggest hut on the site. It was called 'the Barn'. The landlord was a very genial man indeed and made us welcome; he had plenty of spare beds for ninepence a night, he said. He reminded us, however, that if we got a start, he would expect five shillings and sixpence a week in advance. But he was most helpful and lent us knives and forks, tin plates and mugs without handles. He gave us a locker-key each, so now we could solve the food-storage problem. We went to the canteen to get our first supply of groceries.

The canteen stocked everything from a needle to an anchor; one end of the premises also sold bottled beer. But we had a real shock on finding out the prices of food: everything cost twice as much as we had paid in Lancaster. Our funds were now very low. We intended to stick to our bread-and-butter diet for the time being, but after such a hard day we threw discretion to the wind and lashed out on a rasher of bacon and an egg each.

We were just finishing our high tea as the navvies started to arrive from their day's work. These were the real professionals. My friend and I felt a little out of place and a bit humble in their company. Most of them wore moleskin trousers and leather knee-bands, Derby tweed jackets with large pockets, and neckerchieves fastened in a fancy knot at the side of the neck. Their hobnailed boots made a great noise on the wooden floor. There could be only one description for the sleeping accommodation: rough. A row of two-tier bunks lined each side of a long room; we were pleased to be allotted one in a corner. We didn't relish the idea of having a stranger climb down from the top bed in the middle of the night when attending to the calls of nature; we had already noticed the usual large buckets placed at intervals along the floor for this purpose. I think my friend was too tired to climb to the top bed, so I took it. The bedclothes consisted of a straw palliasse and bolster, with four army blankets. This wasn't the height of luxury but, with a freezing wind roaring down the valley like a hurricane, we were glad to have a roof over our heads. Soon we were sleeping the sleep of the just.

The Tosside project came under a number of headings: public works, dam construction and reservoir building.

But the navvies knew it by its ordinary title: waterworks. A concrete barrier of great depth and width was being built across a river from bank to bank. When it was completed, the valley would be flooded and hundreds of acres of what was once arable and grazing land would be submerged forever under millions of gallons of water. Also in the midst of being constructed was a large pipeline which, when the dam was completed, would carry the water supply for the towns and cities of Yorkshire.

Scarcely able to remember where we were, we were roused promptly at 6 am by the switching on of lights; my friend and I got ready to make our first contribution to the Tosside waterworks project, should our services be required. The navvies were soon all up and about: after a spell of yawning, stretching, coughing and spitting, they would dash outside in shirtsleeves and with a towel round their necks, soon to dash back again with reports about the weather. 'By gum, it's reet brass-monkey weather!' reported our neighbour, but we weren't travelled enough to appreciate the subtlety of this remark so early in the morning. Once again the landlord was kind to us and helped us to get our bread-and-butter sandwiches ready in case we got a start. Again our lack of know-how was pitiful: a navvy never speaks of food or sandwiches. In his vocabulary food is known as 'tommy'. We wrapped ours in pieces of old newspaper, while the proper navvies wrapped theirs in neat spotted handkerchiefs. Our first priority from that moment must be to get a white-spotted red handkerchief; the canteen sold them for sixpence. We joined the gangs of men who seemed to pour from each hut on their way to clock-on.

They filed past a half-open window in a long wooden hut, shouted out a number and were given a round metal disc. My friend and I waited until the rush was over before presenting ourselves at the window to inquire if there were any vacancies. A voice inside shouted 'Wait!' and the window was slammed shut. After a few minutes a steam whistle blew a long shrill note, and immediately the whole valley sprang to life. Giant crane-jibs, with steel buckets attached, began to swing to and fro. Railway engines emerged from their sheds and, amidst clouds of steam and black smoke, puffed away in various directions. While we waited to find out what fate had in store for us, we noticed another man nearby. He didn't appear to be looking for work: he looked as if he was already part of the system. Suddenly the window flew open again and a voice said 'Yes?' Before we had time to repeat our request the voice asked: 'Whas yer names? Your hut number? Have ye got insurance cards?' He gave us a metal disc each. 'Don't lose these,' he warned. 'Hand them in each night and collect them each morning. Yer rate of pay is one shilling and three farthings an hour. The working week is fifty hours. But a word of warning: if you are caught smoking on the job during working hours, you will be dismissed on the spot. Go with that gentleman waiting over there,' he ordered. Leaning a bit further out of the window, he shouted, 'Two for you, Dick!' The window was slammed shut again.

We weren't too concerned about the rules and regulations of the job just then; we were far too excited about getting a start. So in single file we followed Dick, who led us for about a half-mile along the edge of the valley, jumping across two or three little streams as we went. Dick – whose full title was Australian Dick – was our ganger man. The only thing Australian about him seemed to be his bush-hat, with one side of the brim curled up and the other side flat over one ear. He was neatly dressed in Derby tweeds, the trousers flared at the bottoms and finished off with many rows of machine stitching.

Eventually we got to our place of work: a big timber structure perched on the side of the hill. At the very top, a gantry carried a light railway; underneath, a large steel-plated chute ran down to the mouth of a massive stone-crusher. Underneath the crusher was another railway line, where a rake of wagons loaded with sand and ballast was waiting for despatch. A diesel engine housed in a nearby shed was the power source for the crusher. My first impression was that all this was a far cry from the old Foden and its crusher which I knew so well back in County Derry.

Yorkshire, of course, is famous for its sandstone. About a mile further north, gangs of men were hard at it in the quarries, keeping the crusher supplied with stone. Being the middle link in the chain between the quarry and the dam wall, our job was to keep the big concrete mixers supplied with sand and ballast. My friend and I brought the strength of Australian Dick's gang up to six. Two were local men; indeed, one was a farmer whose land would be flooded when the dam was completed. Although the other local man must have been in his sixties, he was always referred to as 'Nipper'. He was the tea-boy and general odd-job man. Tea breaks were not permitted on the job; three quarters of an hour at midday was the only break allowed. But Nipper in his quiet way had found a way round the no-tea-break rule. He would drum up at ten in the morning and three in the afternoon every day and bring his scalding brew round in a bucket. In spite of the dust and grit from the crusher, at ninepence a week Nipper's brew was a bargain. The rest of the gang included a man called 'Lank' simply because he came from Lancashire. Another man hailed from either Mayo or Galway (he never told us which) and, although only very young, he was a complete 'loner', hardly ever speaking to anyone. The job allotted to my friend and me was to help this west-of-Ireland man to feed the crusher. Its appetite was insatiable.

We hadn't been going long when a rake of loaded wagons crept along the gantry above us, the buffers just nudging each other until, amid a great hiss of steam, it came to a halt. The wooden framework of the gantry creaked beneath the weight and, taking our cue from the others, we stood well clear. Emptying the wagons was a four-man job, so we followed Dick and scrambled onto the gantry. The wagons were side-tippers, but before they could be emptied the wheels had first to be secured to the rails; this was done by iron grabs which two men held in position. The other two men stationed themselves at each end of the wagon with lifting-poles. After making sure everyone was ready, Dick shouted 'Hi hup!' We all took the strain and up and over she went. There was a terrific crash as the wagonload of rock cascaded down the chute. Then the engine driver's assistant signalled to his mate and the next wagon was gently nudged into position.

At first glance the uninitiated, like my friend and I,

might think that the precautions taken for unloading were a bit overdone. However, when we heard the stories about enthusiasts who, for the sake of showing off, caused serious injury to themselves and endangered the lives of others by attempting to tip wagons single-handed, we understood how necessary the measures were. They would get the wagon up to the point of balance, to find that they could neither bear the weight nor get it over. They would be forced to let go but, not being able to jump clear, would find themselves trapped as the wagon tipped in the wrong direction. Since we were working on the gantry and had nowhere to jump to except the valley below, we began to appreciate the wisdom of Australian Dick's precautions.

The first morning passed very quickly. When the whistle went for our midday break, my friend and I were reminded for the second time that day of our woeful inadequacies as navvies. Not only were the others able to unwrap substantial-looking sandwiches from spotted handkerchiefs, they had billycans as well. They also had small tin canisters with two compartments, with tea and sugar mixed in one compartment and condensed milk in the other. Nipper, however, came to our rescue with a couple of jam jars that helped us over our temporary embarrassment. So now, without fail, as well as a spotted handkerchief, a billycan and a two-compartment canister were absolute essentials. Later in the afternoon a gentleman came striding along the edge of the valley towards us. Apart from wellington boots, he looked like a well-dressed office worker. He was in fact the man who had issued us with the metal discs that morning. He was the timekeeper. The purpose of his visit was to find out if anyone wanted a sub; as far as we two newcomers were concerned, the man and his mission couldn't have been more welcome. We put our names down for five shillings each, which we could draw when we handed in our discs that evening. Subbing was an important feature of the navvies' lifestyle, although it played havoc with the pay packet come Friday. Nevertheless, to newcomers like ourselves, who were almost broke, it gave a temporary sense of security.

By the end of our first day our fingertips began to feel the effects of handling the sandstone and were quite painful, until we discovered that a piece of rubber tubing could be adapted to keep the fingertips covered. When the whistle blew, calling it a day, we hurried off to collect our five shillings, part of our first day's hard earnings as navvies. Now we could think about more substantial meals, so we lashed out on potatoes, sausages and a big hunk of cheese from the canteen. Gradually we became quite expert round the hotplate, and soon we were enjoying meals just as good as the next man's. We discovered that a little planning at the weekend was the key to providing good sandwiches during the week. Boiled bacon or beef were our favourites; we also discovered that a fat bacon sandwich sprinkled with sugar was very tasty indeed.

At weekends, as well as cooking, the navvies spent most of their time washing and mending their clothes, restoring missing buttons and the like. Some had their moleskin trousers so well scrubbed they were almost snow-white. We younger ones could never work up enough enthusiasm for this kind of activity, but then we weren't proper navvies. Sunday was also a day when there seemed to be great competition for the navvy's salvation. It was as if he were some kind of lost soul, wandering in the wilderness, with every religious denomination hell-bent on rescuing him. The Catholics had a small chapel in the middle of the hutments, while almost next door the Church of England had its place of worship. Of the two, the Catholics seemed to have the edge when it came to attendances. On Sunday evenings a section of the canteen was occupied by another sect, which devoted most of its time to hymn-singing. Then there were groups of people handing out religious tracts all over the camp. All this activity, however, helped to pass the time and keep us in touch with the outside world. Otherwise we were completely cut off from the rest of civilisation: there were no newspapers during the week, and radio was unheard of.

As the days grew longer, the first signs of spring began to appear in the valley. Birds began to chirp and sing, and every day more and more little clumps of primroses and posies began to appear along the edges of the streams. The promise of spring brought more men in search of work. Most were professionals who had spent the winter in lodging houses in some town or city but now, during the spring and summer, had to find work which would sustain them when winter came round again. On the day of arrival, some would station themselves near the office, where everyone filed past to hand in their discs. With caps in hands, the new arrivals would collect whatever few coppers anyone cared to donate. It would all help towards securing a bed and a meal of some kind. While dropping a spare copper into some stranger's cap, it didn't take a lot for one to think: 'There, but for the grace of God, go I.'

Most of the new arrivals joined us in the Barn, where accommodation was cheapest. I was now familiar enough with the various accents to distinguish between Lancashire and Yorkshire, where most of them came from. Others came from Tyneside; everyone called them the Geordies and their accent fascinated me. There were also a fair number of Scots and one or two Welshmen, but the Irish were definitely in the minority. So, when the Barn got a bit overcrowded, my friend and I moved to a smaller hut. This was a bit more expensive but there were extra amenities. The beds were single-storey with sheets; the charge was a shilling a night. An evening meal could be had for one and six, and a Sunday dinner for two shillings. For people totally undomesticated like us two, the week's washing could be attended to as well. Since our total weekly income came to only fifty shillings, we couldn't afford to mollycoddle ourselves too much, so we still did most of our own cooking.

Hut management was in the hands of the ganger-men and their families; perhaps it went with the job. K, however, lodged at a local farm. Perhaps he had no family. The general foreman's living quarters were set well apart from the other buildings. He had a trim, neat bungalow surrounded by a well-kept garden. We never had any contact with him but there was no mistaking him, even at a distance. He was always well turned out, his badge of office seeming to be a bowler hat. The navvies always referred to him as the 'Walking Pelter', but he never walked as far as the crusher all the time we were there.

Often we could see his bulky silhouette in the distance against the skyline. Whether or not the rigid no-smoking rule was his or whether someone higher up was responsible for it, we never found out. There certainly weren't any fire risks to be considered, so maybe it was just a question of economics.

Most of the navvies were pipe-smokers, so if a given number of men stopped work to fill their pipes at intervals, this could be considered to be a waste of time in the eyes of the bosses. Australian Dick rolled his own fags and was obviously scared of being caught in breach of the rule. He would hide himself under the crusher, keeping a sharp lookout for anyone approaching. He would take a quick drag from his shag cigarette and hide his hand in the pocket of his Derby tweed jacket. We used to watch the small plume of blue smoke curling up from his pocket.

My friend and I got round the ban by reverting to the old habit of chewing tobacco. At home it was a sign you were growing up if you could chew tobacco without being sick. Wee boys couldn't buy it, so we cadged it; indeed, we were even known to do odd jobs like running errands, just to get a chew of the weed. But if you hung round a man who was filling his pipe, he'd recognise the symptoms immediately and carve you off a sliver of Gallaher's War Horse. Chewing tobacco involved much spitting and encouraged a cruel streak in wee boys in relation to cats. There's nothing a cat likes better than a nice warm in front of the fire. We would take aim with our tobacco spit and hope to get the cat smack in the eye. The effect was immediate: the cat would be out of the house like a streak of lightning and get busy with its paw until the eye ceased to irritate. Come to think of it, cats' eyes seemed to shine much brighter after a bathe in tobacco-spit. Anyway, it helped to keep the dust from the crusher at bay, so perhaps it wasn't an unhealthy habit after all. An ounce of chewing-tobacco called 'pig-tail' coat eightpence and lasted a week. When it got dry and brittle, rolling it in a dock leaf soon restored its original flavour.

Another thing the Walking Pelter kept his eye on was the weather. As soon as the rain started, he would be on the lookout for navvies taking shelter. Then he would signal to the nearest engine driver, who gave a long blast on the whistle. The job would stop, everybody was rained off and the valley become silent again. There was no doubt about it, the Walking Pelter was monarch of all he surveyed and had his own ways and means of being abreast of events on all sections of the job. The old professionals didn't seem to mind being rained off, especially if it happened midweek, when they were ready for another little rest. Back to the huts they would go to drum up and play cards or dominoes. Neither my friend nor I liked the rain-offs: apart from loss of pay, it meant boredom. The professionals were much more philosophical about it, saying: 'It ain't much good making waterworks if it don't rain.'

At the northern end of the dam site stood an old derelict building with a small graveyard at the back. Purely out of curiosity, I went along to see it. The roof and walls were covered in moss and lichen, and slates from the roof had slid out of position and lay where they had fallen, in little piles round the building. The belfry without a bell was crumbling away and looked as if the next gust of wind would demolish it. I wondered if any of its old congregation were still alive but I thought not. The low wall surrounding the graveyard was broken in many places and sheep were using the ruin for shelter. Some of the old headstones were leaning against the wall, with parts of their inscriptions still legible. I noticed there was someone who had been born in the 1790s, but most of the grave-mounds were merely traces, the ground almost level again. Once the dam was completed, the old church would be submerged forever. The graveyard, however, had to be moved. I never found out what the reinterment arrangements were: it was all very hush-hush. In daylight, all I could see was a high canvas screen round the graveyard. A special gang of men worked at night, as flickers from acetylene flares stabbed the eerie darkness of the valley.

17

GOLF AND FIT-BA'

As we came in from work one evening, we were surprised to find about half a dozen young men from around home who had just arrived. They had heard about the job through letters my friend and I had sent home. We must have given the wrong impression, because these fellows came with a different set of expectations altogether. What a miserable lot they were: they didn't like the huts, the job or anyone or anything about the place at all. They almost blamed us for being the cause of the fact that they were there; in any event, they only intended stopping a few weeks before going on the Scotch hay harvest. Next day they all got a start on the pipe track. There was one young fella amongst them who wanted to get to Scotland as soon as possible. He kept urging me to go with him. He had relations living in the Glasgow area, in Cambuslang – or 'Cameslong', as we called it. He was certain these relatives would find us both jobs in no time; then we would be in the big time in the big city. Slogging away on the Yorkshire Moors for a shilling an hour was no life for young fellas like us, he argued, and I was inclined to agree with him.

As it happened, I had a married sister living in Paisley at the time, whom I hadn't seen for a number of years. Probably that was why I got interested in the young fella's suggestion in the first place. Both of us were totally ignorant about the economic climate prevailing at the time, particularly in Scotland. I discussed the idea with my friend but he was entirely non-committal. 'Please yersel'! I won't think any the less of you if you go,' he said. The upshot of it all was that the young fella and I drew our cards, tramped to Hellifield and caught the night train to Glasgow. There was no welcome waiting for us in 'Cameslong': they said we must be mad to leave a job in England and come to Scotland. Half the young fella's relations were already on the 'broo' and the other half would be joining them at the weekend. After this depressing reception, I didn't bother to wait for the cup of tea that was promised. I set off to find my own way to Paisley.

It had been a number of years since I last saw my second-eldest sister. In my mind's eye I still carried a picture of her in the rosy-cheeked winsomeness of her youth. She was so pleased to see me but, alas, the roses had faded and she looked pale and fretful. Her once crowning glory, her jet-black hair, was streaked with grey and looked lifeless. She and her husband and two children were living in a tenement building – known as a 'close' – in Mosside, a stone's throw from St Mirren's football ground. My brother-in-law worked in a local chemical works but he was on tenterhooks: lay-offs were taking place every week and many firms were on a three-day week. In spite of the dismal outlook, however, neither he nor my sister ever hinted that I had made a mistake by coming to Scotland, although they must have known that the General Strike of 1926 was imminent.

I had three or four pounds saved from Tosside. It wouldn't last long but with 'hope in the breast eternal' I believed something would turn up eventually. For some reason or other we Inishowen people were always looked upon as being very independent. We always harboured a great distrust of officialdom and authority, and we would go to great lengths to avoid getting involved with the system. At that particular time, for example, I would rather tramp the country end to end and live on swede turnips than sign on at a labour exchange or hang around on street corners. I once heard my father describe this attitude as being one of 'pride and poverty kicking the arse of us'.

Finding out about job vacancies in Paisley was a case of knowing someone who knew someone. My brother-in-law passed the word around to one or two of his friends, and after about a week I was told there might be a job going on a golf course which was under construction on the outskirts of town. I was to be there at 8 am sharp on Monday morning. When I got there I was surprised to find I was the only applicant for the job. I knew why when I found out that the rate of pay was only eleven pence an hour. Clearly this employer, whoever he was, was taking full advantage of the surplus labour conditions prevailing in Paisley. But no matter, I thought, it was better than nothing – if only just. Beggars can't be choosers, and it would keep me from being a burden to others. I was given a barrow and shovel, and told to wheel sand from a large pile to the various bunkers on the course, which were now in the last stage of completion. There were only two others on the job, and both were Paisley men. The foreman, a very young man, was also in charge of another job somewhere else, so we didn't see much of him. It was fine spring weather and, although the sand was heavy, it was quite pleasant pushing my barrow over the green sward. In the distance I could see vast stretches of the Clyde.

The railway ran past the edge of the golf course at one point and I could see trains packed with soldiers passing at intervals. They were dressed in full fighting gear, as if they were off to war somewhere. Troop movements and rumours of strikes – or anything else, for that matter – were of little interest to the people of Paisley that particular week, For the following Saturday was going to be the most important date in the Scottish calendar: the day of the Scottish FA Cup Final. One of the teams in the final, St Mirren, was based in Paisley; the other team was the legendary Celtic. The other two men with whom I worked talked about nothing but the forthcoming match all week. I had already heard a lot about Celtic; indeed, when football was discussed at home, it was as if the only other two teams in the game, apart from our own team, were Celtic and Rangers. When our own local team took to the field, with only four football shirts between them, the colours were sure to be the white and yellow hoops on the green background.

Before I had finished my first week on the golf course, I got caught up like the rest in cup final fervour and made up my mind to try and get in to the match. I very much wanted to see a professional game and, above all, to see the famous Celtic in action. So on the morning of the great day I just managed to squeeze myself aboard one of the trains that were leaving Paisley every few minutes. While trying to squeeze myself into the carriage, I managed to avoid a deliberate attempt by a railway official to do me a serious injury. A tall, fair-haired man he was, with lots of gold braid on his cap. I was the last one to squeeze into the carriage, keeping my right hand on the outside in order to lever my way forward. As luck would have it, I spotted this man as he grabbed the door handle and, with all the weight of his body against it, slammed the door. I just got my hand clear in time. He may have mistaken me for a Celtic supporter but I was in no doubt about his intention. 'You bastard!' I shouted at him but he just hunched his shoulders a little and pretended to be talking to his mates.

The train never reached its scheduled stopping place. As soon as it slowed down, the carriage doors were flung open and the crowd poured out – down the railway bank, through back gardens and front gardens, across the road in between houses, everyone going full pelt towards what looked like a cinder mountain surrounded by an iron fence. I don't remember paying an entrance fee: among the shoving, pushing and seething mass of people, I found myself being almost carried through the gate. Once inside, I set off with the rest to scramble up the cinder mountain. On reaching the top, I joined the last row of thousands surrounding a patch of green sward. It looked far away down in the hollow and was, of course, the famous Hampden Park. Flags, banners and bunting were draped everywhere, and cheers, roars and rattles kept up an incessant din, while a kiltie band marched and counter-marched on the green turf. The crowd went hysterical as the teams trotted out from a kind of tunnel in the mountain, led by a retinue of officials. Soon the pre-liminaries were over, a coin was tossed, the whistle blew and the battle for the cup was on.

For the first quarter of an hour the game was so fast and furious I just couldn't keep track of it. St Mirren were under pressure, with most of the play concentrated on their half of the pitch. Celtic, with one or two desperate attempts, skimmed the crossbar and rocked the goalposts but failed to find the net. Then, in the twinkle of an eye, the tables were turned. St Mirren broke loose and there was a wild scramble in Celtic's goalmouth. The next thing I saw was the goalkeeper flat on his face while the ball rolled past the end of his fingers into the net.

For a minute or two, the keeper just lay there, kicking the ground with his toes, his head buried in his arms as if to keep out the noise of roars, shouts, cheers and curses, which were deafening. The crowd on the far side of the pitch went berserk, shouting, waving flags and surging from side to side. It was then that I realised I was among Celtic supporters, for they had all gone silent, almost dumbfounded. There was one optimist near me who tried to cheer things up with remarks like 'Never mind! Wee Shooie'll sort the buggers out in the second half.' But from then on the quality of the game began to deteriorate. St Mirren adopted a 'What we have, we hold' attitude: at any sign of trouble, its players fell back and blocked the goalmouth. The ball was kicked out when there was no need to, and as much time as possible was taken to throw it in. The crowd became restive.

The start of the second half was as dull as the end of the first, and soon the barracking, yelling and shouting began. 'Cummon, you bastards, let's have some bliddy fit-ba'. It's enough to gie ye the bluddy scunners, for Christ's sake,' they shouted. Then beer bottles began to land on the pitch. Police, some on horseback and some on foot, began to make their way towards the trouble area. They were met by another fusillade of bottles, lumps of cinder and pieces of wood. While the mêlée was raging, St Mirren abandoned their defensive role and forced a corner on Celtic; the ba' was nodded in and St Mirren got their second goal – and the Cup. In the dying moments I took my cue from someone close by who said: 'Let's get tae hell oota here.' I scrambled down the cinder mountain to the road below, where it looked as if the whole of Glasgow's police were waiting, batons drawn. I didn't really know what to expect from seeing these two professional teams in action, but whatever it was I felt disappointed. I thought if that was professional football at its best, then long live our local team back home, hobnailed boots and steel toe-plates notwithstanding.

18

MAKING HAY . . .

My sand-wheeling job on the golf course lasted exactly three weeks, and the chances of getting another one looked very slim indeed. Scotland was now in the grip of the General Strike. Not being a regular reader of newspapers, I had only a vague idea of what it was all about. I gathered that the coal miners were protesting against wage cuts, and the engineers and railwaymen were backing them up. If this was true, then the whole of Scotland must have been at a standstill. All the factories around Paisley were shut. Groups of men wearing armbands stood about at works entrances; police were everywhere. After the first week, I chanced to see a newspaper headline which proclaimed Glasgow to be in a state of siege. Next day, having nothing better to do, I decided to find out for myself. I boarded a tram at Paisley Cross; the fare to Glasgow was tuppence. Except for two policemen, I was the only passenger until a few people were picked up on the route.

The tram didn't reach its Glasgow terminal: the main thoroughfare was blocked by another tram, which was lying on its side, ablaze. The street was jammed tight with men, and placards and banners were everywhere. The police were trying to break up a demonstration. As they tried to force everyone onto the pavement, the crowd would retreat a few yards and then surge forward again. Men were being batoned to the ground, where they lay and were trodden on. One group was trying hard to prise up cobblestones for use as ammunition. Then there was a clatter of hooves as mounted police charged in to relieve their hard-pressed mates. I managed to squeeze back far enough to join hundreds of others who were to escape down a side street – only to discover that hundreds more were trying to do likewise from the other end, in an effort to get away from a battle in the next street. In the end, I climbed down some steps leading to a tall building, sat down on the top step and waited for the crowd to thin out.

I was cursing myself for getting mixed up in the affray in the first place, and for not realising that there is no such thing as an innocent bystander in those circumstances. If you came within range of a policeman swinging a baton, that was your lookout. Most of the crowd eventually dispersed up the various alleyways. I was roused from my reverie by a policeman shouting: 'Hi, you! Git moving!' The main street looked like a battlefield, littered with stones, bricks and broken glass; a makeshift first-aid post was trying to deal with a crowd of casualties. Picking my way through the debris, I headed back for Paisley on foot.

A week or so later, some of our neighbours, who were local foundry workers, were notified to report back for work. At the same time, a rumour was circulated that there might be half a dozen extra temporary jobs going. Although my brother-in-law knew it would be a waste of time trying for these jobs, there was no harm in going along to find out. We went to the foundry on Monday morning to find a queue of men that reached halfway down the street; half a dozen police were also present. We didn't even bother to cross over. The regular workers used a side entrance to get into the works; then a small door in the main entrance swung open. There was a mad scramble as the first six men jostled with each other to get through the small door. Then the police jumped in and blocked the entrance, and the small door was slammed shut again. The rest of the queue began to disperse in ones and twos. We learned later that the six temporary jobs which had caused all the furore were for unloading pig-iron at a shilling an hour.

To find a job of some kind, somewhere, became most urgent. Even so, I was better off than many others. I had no commitments except to myself, and I was mobile, whereas my brother-in-law had a lovely wife, two lovely children and a place to call home. No doubt he was eligible for some form of unemployment benefit but, like myself, he would take up that option only as a last resort. We Irish tend to be a bit stubborn in this respect: we like to be our own men, beholden to no one. Maybe this is why we tend to undersell ourselves and fail to realise our potential. Although for a variety of reasons Britain has never got round to classifying us as aliens, in our heart of hearts we were and will always remain so. In the end my brother-in-law suggested that the two of us should take a run down to Yorkshire to see if there were any vacancies left in the waterworks at Tosside. If we were unlucky, then we could try for hay-timing in Lancashire. At least it would be better than hanging around waiting for things to improve in Scotland. We decided to travel on a Sunday, aiming to be at Tosside ready to start work, if there was any, first thing Monday morning. I waited outside while he said goodbye to his family. Leave-taking of this kind always saddened me. I was anxious to be on my way but I still recall a little fair-haired boy, a toddler, waving to me from his mother's arms. 'See you to-moddow's day,' he lisped. Alas, I haven't seen him since.

The train seemed to stop at every siding as well as every station; it was late evening before we got to Hellifield and set off to complete the journey on foot. The Yorkshire Moors looked much more pleasant than in February, when I had been caught in a blizzard. Even so, although we didn't know it, there was another hazard in store for us. As soon as the sun went down, the whole landscape became enveloped in a thick, swirling fog. We were on a road, so the only thing to do was to keep going until we found a signpost. At last we came to a crossroads and, after wasting a lot of matches, we read the word 'Slaidburn'. So we trudged on through the misty silence. There didn't seem to be any end to our journey. After about two hours we were getting very tired and fed up, when we came upon another crossroads. We struck more matches to read this signpost: in their sulphur-ous glow we read the word 'Slaidburn' yet again. Oh no, it couldn't be. But it damned well was. We were back at the same crossroads we had a passed a couple of hours before. So we learned that the only sensible thing to do in a fog was to stay put, and we hunkered down in the ditch to wait for it to lift.

The faint rustling of a breeze in the gorse bushes brought us back to life. The fog lifted as quickly as it had come down, the sky became starlit and soon the moors were bathed in bright moonlight as we made a fresh attempt to find Tosside. It wasn't long before we discovered our original mistake: about a hundred yards further on, there was another sign for Slaidburn pointing to the right. We had missed it in the fog. But it was now too late to seek accommodation in the huts at Tosside; we would have to rough it for the night. We approached the dam site from the north side past the quarry. The old tin shed where I used to have my meal-breaks would have to be our shelter for the night. The old church was still there, looking gaunt and lonely in the moonlight; the area inside the low walls had been cleared and it all looked very bare and sad.

In spite of our tiredness we could manage only a fitful doze as we stretched out precariously on the makeshift wooden benches. We hadn't eaten since leaving Paisley and were quite relieved when daylight came. After freshening ourselves up in the little stream I had crossed so often before, we made our way to the office with hope in our hearts. This feeling gave way to grave doubts on finding thirty or more men already there, on the same mission as ourselves. After the whistle blew, the two men nearest dashed to the window and got their metal discs. 'Sorry, no more today,' the timekeeper shouted as he slammed the window shut. So in ones and twos the group dispersed, heading towards Slaidburn, no doubt to tramp to some other job they'd heard about.

Our immediate plan was to stay and keep trying for two more days; then, if there was no luck, we would make for Lancaster. Thursday was market day, and hiring day for hay-timers. Meanwhile, our first jobs were to secure two nights' accommodation and, most urgently of all, a meal of some kind. There were plenty of spare beds in the first hut we enquired at, which wasn't a good sign: it was now well into June and the job should have been going at full blast. But there was a shortage of cement and reinforcing due to the strike, so many sections of the job were closed down. At knocking-off time I wandered down to the office to see if anyone from home, particularly my old companion, was still there. We went to the window where they would be handing in their discs. They had all apparently gone, except for one man, who knew me just as well as I knew him but hurried past without speaking. My brother-in-law and I were outside the office at starting-time for the next two days but nobody was taken on, so we headed for Lancaster.

The market seemed to be very quiet, except for some livestock in pens and an auction in progress: the strike seemed to be casting its shadow here as well. We met a man just arrived from home who was on his way to a farm where he went regularly every year. But he had a bit of a problem, so he was glad to see us. Normally he would have been accompanied by a neighbour but, due to unforeseen circumstances, the neighbour couldn't come, so he was a man short. Would either of us care to go with him? he wanted to know. There was no doubt which one of us should accept the man's offer: my brother-in-law's need was much greater than mine. I knew that as soon as the hay-timing was finished he wanted to be off back to his family. This must have been our lucky day after all: I didn't have to wait long before a farmer came up to me to enquire if I was looking for hay-timing. When I said I was, he invited me to have a glass of beer with him. I had never tasted the stuff before in my life but, since the man was civil enough to ask, it would have been unmannerly to refuse. Also, and more importantly on such occasions, I had enough money to return the compliment.

The crowd in the public house were mostly farmers discussing their favourite topics: the weather, hay prospects and the poor price for livestock. My employer-to-be was anxious to know if I could use the scythe. I took great pleasure in assuring him that, scythe-wise, I was his man. He complained rather sadly that his scything days were over: his back had gone, he said. Looking at him, I could see what he meant. He was a heavily built man in his sixties and moved with a permanent stoop. The bad back is a common enough complaint among farmers; how much of this is due to their way of life or just to sheer neglect, it's difficult to assess. No amount of time and expense is spared on a sick animal, and rightly so; when it comes to themselves, however, they can't spare the time or the money. 'Who would look after things in my absence?' is the usual get-out: maybe it's just an excuse for a little bit of martyrdom. Anyway, I enjoyed my first pint of ale, even if I didn't like the taste of the stuff. My brother-in-law and his friend were still waiting for their boss to pick them up. But we did have a chance to exchange addresses and agree to contact each before making any fresh moves.

My boss reappeared with his horse and cart to say he was ready to go home, so we climbed aboard. He told me he had sold two calves at the auction – or, as he put it, he had almost given them away. Perhaps the calf money covered my wages, which were six pounds for a month or until the hay was finished within that period. It all depended on the weather: we might be lucky and three weeks would do it. However, six pounds for a month was an improvement on six pounds for six months in County Derry; at least it appeared to be at the time. My new boss was quite affable and I learned a lot about him and his family on the way to his home, which was somewhere off the main road between Lancaster and Garstang. It was a small family: himself and his wife, and a son and daughter. But the son wasn't much help to him at that time, being a full-time student at an agricultural college. According to the father, his son was just a book farmer. The wife and daughter were his sheet anchor, as he said: he could never manage without them.

I wondered what the unusual smell was that assailed my nostrils as we entered the farmyard. The boss was very proud to show me where the smell emanated from – a 'cheese mountain', the like of which I had never seen before nor since. A Dutch barn stood behind the farmhouse, stacked to the roof with rolls of cheese. It had all been sold, the boss told me, and he was hoping it would be collected soon, because he was getting short of space. Meanwhile the dogs and cats slept on it and piddled all over it, the hens laid their eggs on it and later I scrambled all over it. So tough was the outer skin, my hobnailed boots never made a mark on it. After an informal introduction to the two women, who were most pleasant indeed, we had a meal and then the boss proceeded to get his mowing machine ready. I could see he was anxious to make a start. Would I get the scythe and open the field across the road, he asked.

Now, the scythe is very much a one-man weapon: it would be impossible to hang the blade of a scythe to suit anyone except the user. Yet the method of setting the blade was very simple. Holding the scythe by the handles and standing up as straight as possible, you stretched the right leg until the toe of the boot touched the tip of the blade, which was then fastened. A badly set blade was about as useless as an Indian club for mowing hay. Nineteen twenty-six was a great year for hay: farmers couldn't remember when they'd had a better crop and such ideal weather for saving it. As soon as I had opened the first field, the boss was there with his pair of horses and an old Ransome mower. He followed me from field to field until the mowing was finished.

The working hours were from dawn to dusk. The weather was so hot that we had to keep the hay on the move to avoid its becoming bleached. The secret was to secure it while it still contained a high percentage of its own moisture. But it was thirsty work and for the first day or two I nearly made myself ill by consuming large quantities of home-made lemonade. This was brought to the field in a bucket by one of the women and placed in the shade of the hedge with a nice white cloth on top. The more I visited the bucket, the more thirsty I became – it was that old sweet tooth again – until I was going around with a belly as tight as a drum. As far as food was concerned, however, I was well looked after: this family kept a good table, which I shared with them. The hay was secured in three weeks. Baling wasn't a common practice in those days and it was considered sufficient to stack the hay loose in Dutch barns. Then I had a visit from my brother-in-law, who had already finished and had made arrangements with a long-distance lorry driver for a lift back to Glasgow. When we said 'So long', we didn't know it was the last time we would see each other.

19

TUNNEL TIGER

Now I was on my own and had to decide what was going to be my next move. There was no point in going back to Tosside. The only place I could think of where work might be available was north Wales, which I had heard the navvies at Tosside discussing on a number of occasions. It wasn't much of a job, by all accounts: conditions were rough and, with the pay at a shilling an hour, there was a continual turnover of labour. I decided to give it a try, so I collected my hard-earned hay money and headed for Lancaster. From there, I took the train to Wrexham, from where, still sticking to the navvy principle of not spending too much money on public transport, I would finish the journey on foot.

I was well clear of Wrexham when the evening started to draw in. I was keeping an eye out for a suitable barn where I could rest for the night. The weather was good enough for sleeping in a hedge but I preferred a roof of some kind over my head if possible. Nevertheless, caution was necessary: the law of trespass, and worse, was ever waiting for the unwary. I had heard the navvies at Tosside talk about their tramping experiences. They were experts and had their own vocabulary of do's and don't's when on the road. Once it got dark and you were dead beat, there was a great temptation to crawl into the nearest barn to rest your weary head and feet, forgetting that the first thing a farmer does in the morning is let his dogs out. As soon as the dogs pick up the scent, they'll be prancing round the barn, barking their heads off. Soon the farmer will arrive with his pitchfork and start prodding the hay. I had heard one or two navvies describe their narrow escapes from the business end of a pitchfork. The next-biggest hazard for a man on the road was the police. Some time later I had the experience of being questioned by the police and I was left with the impression that in their books a man on the tramp is a vagrant and the lowest form of social outcast. If he happens to speak with an Irish accent, he is a potential criminal as well.

But it was nearly dark now. I was well out in the country before I noticed the outline of a Dutch barn in a field about 200 yards from the road. It was dark enough for me to approach it unobserved. It was half full of last year's hay; this would do me for the night. I slept well and at almost first light I was back on the road again, minding my own business. I passed through one or two villages but nowhere could I obtain a cup of tea. Eventually I came across a small bakery, so I had to make do with a couple of buns for the time being. It was well into the afternoon when I arrived at my destination: the small village of Dolgarrog, lying at the west end of the Ffestiniog valley.

The Dolgarrog job was one of reconstruction. A few years earlier, the wall of an old dam had given way: millions of tons of water swept over the edge of the mountain, striking the unsuspecting village below. Most of the village was destroyed and many lives were lost. Strange as it may seem, the contractor who was constructing the new dam was the same firm that had built the old one. The works site was on a plateau high above the village. The only way to get up to it was by climbing a zigzag path up the mountainside. There was also a light-gauge railway, used for transporting supplies from the village to the site, that was powered by a steam winch; a steel hawser was attached to two wagons and the empty wagon going down pulled the loaded one up. Both wagons met midway, where a switching arrangement allowed them to pass each other. If you had a head for heights you could ride on them at your own risk. They weren't operating the day I arrived, so I climbed the mountain.

To say the living conditions on the work site were rough would be an understatement. 'Primitive' would be a better description. A few old weather-beaten huts were scattered about haphazardly near the edge of the mountain. I enquired about accommodation at the first hut I came to: there were plenty of beds at a shilling a night. I obtained a few groceries at the canteen and paid an exorbitant price. I was in the process of drumming up my first cup of tea that day, when a gentleman entered the kitchen and said he had seen me struggling up the mountain. By the look of him, he wasn't a navvy: he wore a collar and tie, and had highly polished boots and leggings. I presumed he was one of the office staff. One of his hands was missing and had been replaced by a shiny steel hook. Did I fancy going to work straight away, he enquired: one of the tunnel gangs was short of a muck-shifter. The nightshift started at 6 pm. A good night's sleep would have suited me much better but there was no point in looking a gift horse in the mouth. So I said yes.

The tunnel paid the highest rates on the job: one and thruppence an hour for muck-shifting, as against a shilling an hour on the rest of the job. Armed with a slip of paper for the ganger-man of the nightshift, I picked my way across the boulder-strewn bed of the old dam site, looking for the hole in the mountain that was the tunnel mouth. The mountain tops of that part of north Wales were a labyrinth of dams, tunnels and pipetracks. It was the main source of a cheap water supply for many parts of England, particularly the west Midlands and Merseyside. I noticed one or two others heading in the same direction as myself, so I took my time and followed them to the tunnel mouth, where the ganger-man – or the 'quare fella', as he was called – was waiting.

At six o'clock sharp, six or seven men emerged from somewhere in the bowels of the mountain: the dayshift. Their clothes and faces were covered with white stone-dust, as if they had come out of a flour mill. They looked ageless. By their accents, I concluded they all came from the south of Ireland, and in fact they were all Kerrymen. Each shift ended with a blasting operation to ensure that there was plenty of work waiting for the new shift. Following the others, I made my way to the tunnel face, which was still wreathed in a cloud of dust. One or two light bulbs were strung out along the tunnel, which because of the layer of dust was in semi-darkness. Airlines and cables of various kinds lay or hung in festoons everywhere, and a narrow-gauge railway ran down the centre of the tunnel. But this was no occasion for sightseeing; a large pile of rock and rubble was waiting for disposal. So, with sledgehammers and shovels, two other men and myself went to work loading wagons. Just ahead of us, two pneumatic drills went into action, and the noise in this confined space was ear-splitting. The drillers – or machinemen, as they were called – were the highest-paid men in the gang, on one and ninepence an hour. Wrestling with a pneumatic drill on a rock face for a twelve-hour shift separated the men from the boys. But the two fellas in this gang seemed to take it in their stride. They were twin brothers in their early twenties and hailed from Galway.

What I considered to be the easiest job went to two local Welshmen: one trundled the wagons back and forth with a small diesel engine, while the other kept the tip tidy. Both were very quiet men indeed and, when they did converse with each other, it was always in their native language. As far as tunnel gangs go, we were a mixed bag. Normally it is a family or group of friends and relations who make up a tunnel gang. Apart from the worst possible working conditions, there was always an element of danger on the job. The extra money gave tunnel-men a little extra status; compared with the ordinary navvy, they considered themselves tough and liked being referred to as the tunnel tigers. Our ganger-man was very keen indeed: it was his first chargeship and as yet he hadn't made up his mind whether to become one of 'them' or remain one of 'us'. Meanwhile, he was trying to hustle things along, so perhaps he had made up his mind.

I discovered later that there was a bonus scheme in operation and that the ganger-man was the main bene-ficiary. Perhaps this was why he was always trying to set the pace. I never found out if any of the others received any extra money but those most entitled to it would have been the machinemen. It was on their skill and determination that the progress of the work depended. However, no extra money came my way – not that I expected any – although I was carrying my two mates and they were leaning on me hard. I had much sympathy for the elder of the two. Although only in his forties, his health was ruined. Frequently he would have to lean against the side of the tunnel to get his breath back, and he was also very deaf. Years of exposure to stone dust in quarries and tunnels was killing him. He was, however, an expert in the use of explosives, and the ganger-man relied heavily on his expertise. The other man was a different kettle of fish: he was just bone idle. Both the men and the ganger-man were 'townies', so, being the youngest of the trio and an outsider, I just had to get on with it.

The twin brothers from Galway were great characters, always challenging each other to a 'running jump'. There was a deep ravine running down the mountainside near the tunnel, which we crossed by a little footbridge. But when the twins felt like it, with caps in hand and a 'hey oop' they would take a flying leap across the ravine and roll down the mountainside, laughing like children. To think of this after a twelve-hour stint on the tunnel face was a challenge to the stoutest heart. I think the older men envied the twins their exuberance, as they stood on the footbridge watching. 'Aw, Jaysus, will ye jist look at the two buck-goats from Galway,' one would say. But like the rest of us, the twins were there only for the money. When they had saved enough for their fares, they would be off to Boston, where they had many relatives and good jobs waiting for them. Or so they said.

Working at night had few compensations, although at the tunnel face there was little difference between day and night. It was a twilight world. Yet somehow it didn't seem right to be slogging away while the rest of the world was abed – although there was no social life to be considered. Very few ventured down from the mountain top until it was time for them to move on somewhere else. Being the only occupant of the hut during the day, at least I got a good day's sleep. Saturday night, when the shift wasn't working, was the only occasion when I came into contact with the rest of the inmates. On Saturday afternoons I would catch the steam-winch train on its last run down to the village. There was a fairly frequent train service to Portmadoc, where I did my weekend shopping. Not only was this an excuse for me to get back to civilisation, but I also very much resented the exorbitant prices charged for foodstuffs in the canteen. The navvies were captive customers: they paid the price charged or went without. The next thing that deterred all but one or two from going down to the village was getting back up again. Not only was it a long haul up the zigzag path, it could also be treacherous in the dark.

There was another way up, of course, but having done it once I decided that it was a case of once only, never again. It was a Saturday night just after dark when I arrived back at the village with my little bit of shopping, and I was about to tackle the zigzag path when I bumped into the twins. There they were, having just tossed a coin to decide if they would go up the path or crawl up the steam-winch rails. The penny came down heads, of course, so the issue was decided. 'Come on, Dev, the last man up buys the beer,' they said. I was never sure whether bravado was a sign of foolishness, fear or even cowardice, but it can get you involved in some ridiculous situations. That was how I felt as I set off behind the twins. The first fifty yards or so were nothing – just walking on the sleepers. From there on, however, the rails began to part company with terra firma, and in between the supporting gantry struts there was nothing but darkness. Now there was only one thing to do: keep going forward. It was too dark to see how the twins were making out, though they still kept up a continuous banter between themselves, with the odd 'Are you still there, Dev?' shouted at me.

By now I had spreadeagled myself with a leg on each rail, pulling myself forward with both hands. But at this altitude the rails were beginning to catch the frost and become slippery, and my hands were numb. For good measure my Sunday joint in an old kitbag would swing from one shoulder to the other, giving me a good clout on the ears as it did so. But we had reached the point of no return and there was nothing for it except to keep going, as the rails got higher and higher above the tall trees growing on the mountainside. Our predicament became more hazardous when at one point we discovered that the steel hawsers passed through a bath of wagon-grease, which we had to crawl over. The last ten yards seemed to be almost vertical; trembling, exhausted and shaking like aspens, we crawled off the rails and lay on the ground until we could get our breath back. For once, the twins were speechless.

20

THE BOO-GEERS OF TRAWS

As at Tosside, hut management was in the hands of the gangers and their families, who in the main were Scots. Some, as in the hut I was in, employed a deputy, a kind of jack of all trades. He kept the hotplate going and the place tidy; he answered queries, settled arguments and generally made himself responsible for law and order. Saturday nights were generally the time when rows would flare up. Most of these were the result of sheer boredom but they helped to relieve the monotony. Card-playing and beer were the only forms of relaxation at weekends. Bottled beer could be obtained in the hut at any hour of the day or night: it was sold in unlabelled bottles at a shilling and a penny a time, which was at least double the price charged in pubs. When arguments developed to the stage of 'We'll settled this outside', the outcome could be very interesting indeed.

Much depended on how many thought it worthwhile to go outside and watch. It was no good going to all that trouble without an audience: the rest of us would never know who the best man was. If there was no audience, the two pugilists would just give each other a shove, call each other a few names, sneak back to the hut and stand each other another round of beer. On the odd occasion when the fight looked like getting out of hand, the deputy would intervene. He was a Scot and always looked like the fairground character in the boxing booth who challenges all-comers. His head seemed to be not only clean-shaven but highly polished as well. A singlet, trousers and a pair of plimsolls was all I ever saw him dressed in. When he considered it was time to stop the fight, he would grab both fighters and shake them like a dog shakes a rabbit. 'Och! Awa' back tae yer beer. My oul granmither could knock the shite outa the pair o' ye!' he would say. So it was back for another round of beer, with one for the deputy.

After about two months, rumour had it that the nightshift was being withdrawn. I wasn't too concerned about this, as I had long since come to the conclusion that I just wasn't cut out for a tunnel career. Even after a few weeks I didn't like the look of myself at all: the bloom was fading and I was getting as pale and pallid as the rest of my tunnel companions. According to the ganger-man, the gang wasn't to be dispersed: it was to go shaft-sinking instead. We would be tunnelling vertically instead of horizontally: the same difference, only to my mind much more dangerous. Shafts are an essential part of tunnel construction and are usually sited midway between the tunnel mouths; they are the control-points. There was one already in the course of construction on another site. I made a point of going along one day, just to see what conditions were like.

I found a large circular hole in the ground, wreathed at ground level in a thick layer of stone dust. Away down in the depths somewhere, I could hear pneumatic drills boring away. A large crane was situated some distance from the mouth of the shaft, its driver being directed by a banksman standing at the edge of the dust-cloud. The only means of communication between the shaft-sinkers and the banksman was a handbell, which was rung when the skip was full and ready for hauling to the surface. I watched the skips come hurtling out of the dust-cloud loaded with rock and rubble, while the empty skips went plummeting down to the shaft-bottom at top speed. I got to wondering what chance of escape there was at the shaft-bottom, should anything go wrong. Protective headgear to guard against falling debris was unheard-of in those days. So I decided there and then that shaft-sinking wasn't my scene at all.

Further east along the Ffestiniog valley, another new dam site was under construction near the village of Trawsfyndd. The navvies called it 'Traws'. There was a continuous turnover of labour between Dolgarrog and the new dam site. I heard there were some men from around home working at Traws, so when the nightshift was withdrawn I jacked up and headed for the new site. I made the short journey in comfort: in those days a train consisting of a couple of carriages used to wind its way along the edge of the valley at regular intervals, stopping at villages with unusual names like Llanrust, Betws-y-Coed and Blaenau-Ffestiniog, home of the famous slate quarries. The new dam site was much nearer to civilisation than the mountain top at Dolgarrog and straddled the bottom of the valley. Many acres of farmland would be submerged once the dam was completed. The village of Trawsfyndd is steeped in Welsh history, its people entirely Welsh-speaking. It is also the birthplace of one its famous poets, a shepherd named Evans, whose bardic name was Hedd Wyn. He was awarded the poet's chair in 1917 but, alas, the award turned out to be posthumous: he had been killed in France a few weeks earlier.

The wooden huts where the navvies lived seemed to be a bit more modern than those at Dolgarrog; perhaps being on low ground made the surroundings look less desolate. I made myself a meal and waited for the crowd to come in from work, to see if there was anybody I knew. There were one or two. But much to my surprise, a stranger approached me and asked if I fancied a bit of a night work. For the second time in Wales, I was offered a job without asking.

'The boo-geers are a man short,' the stranger said.

'The boo-whaters?' I queried, suspecting some kind of leg-pull.

'Test-borers,' the man said. 'They only work at night. It's a cush number,' he continued. 'Tell them Barney sent you.'

I was still a bit dubious but there was only one way to find out. With a cheese sandwich just in case, I set off to find the 'boo-geers'.

I came across a small gang of men working at the bottom of a very deep trench. High on the bank, a crane-driver was perched in a little cabin on top of his machine, and a very youthful-looking banksman was wrestling with a skipful of rubble, trying to get it into the emptying position.

'Is the gaffer about?' I queried.

'In there,' the banksman replied, nodding in the direction of an old tin hut.

The ganger-man was elderly but with all the hallmarks of the professional navvy about him, as he sat on a bench filling his pipe, a bottle of beer beside him.

'A man named Barney told me you were a man short,' says I.

'Got your cards?' he asked. Then he shouted up to the banksman, 'Take this young fella across and show him the job.'

'Ye'll need these!' said the banksman, picking up a large bass broom and a couple of wire brushes.

I followed him down two or three leats of very shaky ladders to the trench-bottom. As we scaled the rock face on the other side, he told me he was a Mayo man. On the rock ledge two men were setting up drilling machines. 'I brought you some help,' said the Mayo man. One of the drillers just nodded. 'When yer not helping these fellas, you can get on with this job,' said the Mayo man as he picked up the end of a hosepipe and demonstrated how to hose down the rock face. The bass broom and the wire brushes were to be used for getting all the muck and clay out of the nooks and crannies.

Meanwhile the two drillers needed a hand with their machines. Drills of all sizes, from two to twenty feet, were strewn around everywhere. Both men wore collars and ties, stout wellington boots and nice warm-looking donkey jackets with the words 'Engrs: Office' painted in bold white letters across the back. These two men weren't just ordinary navvies: they were in fact the 'boo-geers'. I was rubbing shoulders with the elite. Both were local men and they always conversed between themselves in their native tongue. But the three of us got along all right. The drills were much easier to handle than those the tunnel-men had to use. Mounted on a tripod, all the driller had to do was turn a handle, which kept the drill in position as it bored its way downwards. One of my jobs was to spray water round the drill, in an effort to clear the dust, which would ooze and splash up in a kind of slurry. Even so, it was very much a trial-and-error operation, and sometimes the drill would get stuck fast and no amount of coaxing would shift it. So it was really a fifty-fifty operation: for every hole we got to the required depth, there was another with a drill jammed solid in it. Now and then, when the driller wanted to discuss something with his mate, I would be asked to take over. I liked this but, erring on the side of caution, I took things very steadily. I didn't want to be the one who got a drill jammed.

My knowledge of engineering standards for dam construction was very rudimentary indeed but gradually I found out what the 'boo-geeing' exercise was about. We were testing the rock formation for flaws and weak spots before the concrete barrier was laid down. Once a series of holes was drilled, they were all plugged and hermetically sealed, except one. Compressed air was applied to the unsealed hole and a pressure meter fitted. After a period of time, any loss of pressure would register on the meter, indicating flaws in the rock. The theory was that, if air can escape, so can water.

As far as navvying goes, and certainly compared with tunnel work, 'boo-geeing' wasn't a bad job at all. I was getting one and a penny an hour, compared with a shilling, which was the standard rate on the job. As far as the ganger-man was concerned, I was under the jurisdiction of the 'boo-geers', and as far as they were concerned I was just a navvy helper. So, being nobody's baby, I was able take advantage of my anonymity and make the best of both worlds. About one in the morning, the two Welshmen used to disappear somewhere for a meal break. In their absence, I would get on with the rock scrubbing. It was very cold in the small hours of the morning in those Welsh valleys; there was no protective clothing for navvies, so the only way to keep warm was to keep moving.

At meal-break time the rest of the gang used to forgather in an old tin shed, where a makeshift bench was arranged for seating accommodation. An old coke brazier stood at the entrance, giving off its foul-smelling sulphuric fumes. Of them all, the young fella from Mayo was the most affable. He appeared to have the full run of the job: besides his banksman's duties, he looked after a steam pump and maintained the acetylene flares that gave us light. I discovered later that the navvies didn't have much time for anyone who appeared to have the run of the job. They were known as the 'blue-eye' or the foreman's 'kiddie', and it was taken for granted that they were getting a penny or two extra an hour for being the eyes and ears of the ganger-man. For all that, our friend from Mayo had a personality so pleasant that it belied the suggestion that he might be in the foreman's pocket.

At one end of the dam site a tunnel was under construction and one of the tunnel gangs was made up entirely of one family of six brothers. They came from a place near home, called Ballymagan. The eldest brother was the ganger-man and the youngest the tea-boy. What a tough bunch they were. It was said they could double their basic pay by bonus payments. Bonus schemes of one kind or another were operated where the going was tough, particularly in dangerous areas like tunnels. Many believed that chasing the bonus was the main cause of many accidents: corners would be cut and safety precautions ignored in order to push the job forward. Then, when an accident occurred, invariably it would be some unsuspecting navvy who would be the victim, as on the morning we all downed tools and ran like hell in the direction of screams which came from somewhere near where the crane was working. It was pitch black as we slid and slithered down the rock face to the trench bottom. There were so many of us trying to climb the shaky ladders all at once it was a wonder the ladders didn't collapse, but nobody gave it a thought.

In the flickering light of an acetylene flare, all we could see at first was an empty skip hanging on two sling-chains swinging to and fro. The screaming had stopped. Just over the edge of the rubble tip, wedged in a gully among the rocks, lay the young fella from Mayo, pinned down by a large boulder. Not knowing what to do for the best, our first reaction was one of helplessness. Fortunately, the old ganger-man had the good sense to send someone running to the village for a doctor. Meanwhile we realised that the first thing to do was to get the weight off the man's body. But how? Even if we had the strength, there wasn't room for enough of us to get round the boulder and lift it.

There wasn't time to think about digging a pathway on the other side of the gully, so that the boulder had a clear run once we got it on the move. Somehow three of us got our hands and shoulders to the massive piece of rock. The first mighty heave not only relieved the dead weight from the young fella's body but gave room for the others to help us send the horrible piece of rock hurtling down to the bottom of the rubble tip.

It didn't seem possible that the young fella could still be alive, for none of us could imagine how the human body could endure so much punishment. 'Christ, I wish that doctor would hurry up,' the old ganger-man kept saying. Meanwhile, we gathered all the old coats and cement bags – anything that would hold any heat that was left in the fella's body – and wrapped them round him. Although it was only a quarter of an hour, it seemed hours before two men, one carrying a rolled-up stretcher, made their way towards us with the aid of a flash lamp. One, obviously the doctor, got down on one knee in the rubble, flashed his torch in the lad's face and opened the closed eyelids. He took a syringe from his case and, pushing the sleeve of the lad's jacket up as far as possible, sank the needle into the lad's forearm. 'We need a sling,' he said, raising himself from the rubble. 'A couple of jackets will do.' Another man and myself took off our jackets and, with the doctor saying, 'Careful, gently, steady,' we eased them under the Mayoman's body. Some of the others steadied us as we carried our burden on to level ground and the stretcher.

The first grey streaks of dawn were beginning to break through the blackness of the Welsh mountain tops as the stretcher party set off, scrambling over the rocks and rubble towards the village. As soon as they had gone, the rest of us simply said: 'To hell with the work.' Someone drummed up and we all sat around in the old tin shed, holding our own inquest on the accident. The only person who had seen what had happened was the crane driver, but then he had been perched up in his cabin and, the only light being an acetylene flare, he just couldn't be sure of what he'd seen. The men at the trench bottom sent up the lump of rock simply because they couldn't reduce it any further with sledgehammers; a slab of gun cotton was needed to blow the rock apart but there was none available. The rock was crowbarred onto the skip and so this lethal load was hauled up to our young unsuspecting friend the banksman. When he went to empty it, it rolled in the wrong direction and the lad was trapped.

We sat around in the old shed, drinking scalding tea and smoking, until it was time to gather up the tools. Meanwhile, all we could do was keep our fingers crossed for our friend from Mayo. It was three days before we got any news. The old ganger-man had a message to say that our friend was still alive and responding slowly to treatment. But he would be a hospital patient for a long, long time. In those days there were no safety regulations that could be legally enforced; there was no liability against employers and no compensation for victims. Not only were the navvies a cheap labour force, they were also expendable.

As at Dolgarrog, most of the ganger-men and hut-managers at Traws were Scots. This arrangement seemed to be the policy of this particular firm of contractors.

Most public-works contractors were still family names; consortiums and multinationals were unheard of in those days. But the firm we were working for in Wales appeared to find the efforts of the Scots and Irish most rewarding indeed. It was said that the head of the firm, when replying to a toast given in his honour, said: 'Give me Scots ganger-men and Irish navvies and I'll make the deserts bloom.'

21

GUARDSMAN

As indicated in the introduction, the material in this book was selected from my uncle's original manuscript. These first seventeen chapters represent the first 118 pages of his typescript which describe his childhood, youth and early manhood. The remaining chapters have been fashioned from later periods of his life and are necessarily discontinuous. He kept on working as a tramping navvy in Leeds and other parts of Yorkshire. He managed to come home for his father's funeral but soon returned to England and found what work he could. There seemed no reason to change this pattern of existence but then, as he puts it himself, you never know what's round the corner.

At least for the time being, it didn't look as if I was going to make any change in my lifestyle at all, and I had more or less resigned myself to carrying on navvying. But then you never know what's round the corner. It was now late autumn and a spell of wet weather had set in; the rain-offs became more frequent and many navvies were 'jacking up' and heading for the towns, where they would spend the winter. One day when the job was completely rained off I tidied myself up and went for a look round. Having spent one winter in Leeds, I fancied a change, so I visited Bradford and Wakefield and for some unknown reason finished up in Halifax.

The thought of having to spend the winter in any of these places on my own wasn't very exciting and left me feeling a bit despondent about life in general. I stood for a while watching a policeman on point duty directing traffic at a street crossing. During a lull I went across and asked him if there was a recruiting office about. He looked at me quizzically for a moment and then, after waving his arms a time or two, said: 'Thinking of taking the plunge, are you? I don't blame you,' he added. 'Not much around for young fellas these days. What were you thinking of joining?' At that moment I hadn't the faintest idea, until I thought of old Jack's Guards. 'Yes,' said the policeman, 'if you fancy hanging around London and spending most of your time in guardrooms. If I was you, I'd go for a bit more excitement, get abroad, see the world. Anyway, good luck to you! The recruiting office is at the barracks up the hill there.'

I trudged on up the hill and the nearer I got to the sprawling buildings on the top, the more doubtful I became. But the word 'London' that the policeman had mentioned added a new dimension to my thoughts. There was nothing to prevent me from turning back, yet I kept on going until I reached the main gate. The place looked very much like what I imagined a prison to be. The soldier on duty at the gate directed me to the recruiting office.

He had a wry smile on his face, as if to say, 'There's one born every minute.'

In answer to my knock, a voice said 'Come in!' An elderly-looking soldier sitting behind a desk asked, 'What can I do for you?'

When I had stated my business, he rose from his desk and announced that the minimum height was 5 foot 11. 'Stand over here,' he ordered, at the same time almost pushing me towards the wall. A piece of wood clonked me on the head as he read off the height scale. 'You'll do! With a bit to spare,' he announced.

'Right, then! We'll have a few particulars,' said he, smoothing out an exhaustive-looking questionnaire on his desk. When he came to date of birth, I hesitated a moment before adding an extra year to my age; goodness knows why.

'You don't seem to be too sure,' queried the soldier. 'All right, let me put it another way. How old will you be on your next birthday?' he asked.

'Eighteen,' said I.

'When is your next birthday?' he asked.

'March,' I replied. At last the questionnaire was completed to his satisfaction.

'You still want to join the Guards?' he asked.

'Yes,' said I.

'The snag is,' he continued, 'there are no vacancies at the moment but if you change your mind I can fix you up straight away.' He named a long list of army units.

But, seeing the 'no vacancies' as a way out, I dug my heels in and said, 'No, it's the Guards or nothing.'

'Are you working?' the soldier asked. I told him I was.

'All right, we'll have to leave it like that. I'll write to you when I get the go-ahead. Good day to you.'

As I hurried out of the barracks and down the hill again, I was quite pleased with myself and thought I'd had a close shave. So the next time my future came up for discussion back on the job, I would be able to look old Jack straight in the eye and say: 'They wouldn't have me in your Guards, Jack. They're not taking any more on.' What the recruiter omitted to tell me was that 'no vacancies' applied only to the depot training programme; there was no room for more recruits *for the time being*. Then I took comfort in the belief that perhaps as the weeks went by the army would forget all about me. I didn't realise that, like the elephant, the army never forgets.

I never breathed a word to a soul about my day in Halifax until one evening two or three weeks later when I was waiting at the counter for my dinner. 'Oh, that reminds me,' said Big Rosie, the site cook, 'I've got a letter for you somewhere, young 'un.' Rummaging in her overall pocket, she fished out a buff-coloured envelope marked 'OHMS'.

'What have you been up to?' she asked under her breath. But there was no point in trying to keep my secret any longer. The short, terse letter ordered me to report back to the barracks at Halifax by 9 am the following Monday morning, en route to the Guards depot somewhere in the south of England.

The contents of the letter soon became public knowledge: the bloke behind me in the dinner queue had already read it over my shoulder. 'Ha, ha!' he shouted to all and sundry, 'I'm buggered if young Pad hasn't gone and done it now: he's joined the bloody Guards, no less.'

'Sarves him bloody right,' was the next comment.

'Leave the lad alone, it's nowt to do wi' you!' said Big Rosie.

'There'll be no "Do you want another pudding, dear" next week,' someone else remarked.

'Huh! He'll be lucky to get a dinner, never mind a pudding, from that bloody lot,' remarked another one.

'Take no notice, Pad boy, they're only jealous 'cos they're all short arses,' said Jack.

For all the banter and leg-pulling, I knew that when Monday morning came I was going to miss these men, whose ways I was getting used to. They had their own special blend of camaraderie that was probably unique. Also, in spite of all the hard graft and the ups and downs, there was a certain amount of individual freedom about the life. No commitment or job-loyalty was called for: I could jack up and hit the road anytime I felt like it. But even in those far-off days, the navvy as a breed was beginning to disappear. Mechanisation was taking over and one man with a mechanical digger could shift more muck in an hour than two or three gangs of navvies could in a whole day. But it was the men with their picks and shovels who laid the foundations of industrial Britain; they were the unsung heroes and the guerrillas of the Industrial Revolution. Although they built the roads and railways and dug the canals, their contribution to society was rarely mentioned. On the odd occasion when they were mentioned, they were usually portrayed as a bad lot: drunken, foul-mouthed, lazy and totally God-forsaken. Alas, there never seemed to be anyone around at the time to rebut this slanderous condemnation.

It was left to a west Donegal man, Pat MacGill, a navvy himself, to highlight and record the exploitation of this cheap labour force. He covered the navvy scene in Britain before going to America, to find the life of the navvy there even more desperate. Sadly, as I write this, all his books have long been out of print; one, however, *Children of the Dead End,* will always remain a classic. MacGill's books, like those of many others to follow him, were banned in Ireland, not because his work was blasphemous or obscene but for something which the guardians of morality considered far more dangerous. He attacked what he believed to be a conspiracy between Church and State to use emigration as a safety valve, in order to keep things quiet in Ireland. He denounced the system that every year forced thousands of young people onto the highways and byways of the world, to be forgotten as though they had never existed. That was Pat MacGill's crime, for which his native land had him declared *persona non grata.*

'Don't forget you've got to be up early in the morning, young 'un,' warned Big Rosie as she handed me my last cup of cocoa on Sunday night. I didn't forget and neither did she: we were the only ones astir long before daylight. There was enough breakfast on my plate for two men. 'Don't leave any, you might not get a chance of another meal today,' she warned. I finished the breakfast and started dithering about, going back to my cubicle pretending I had forgotten something. In the end Rosie propelled me towards the door. 'You'll miss that bus if you don't hurry,' said she, her bottom lip a-tremble. 'Don't forget to come and see us when you get a chance!' she called after me. I waved but didn't look back.

The recruiter was waiting for me when I arrived at the barracks in Halifax. 'Wait here a moment!' he ordered as he disappeared into an office. It wasn't long before his head reappeared at the door. 'Right, in you come!' he ordered. A man whom I took to be an officer rose from behind his desk and in a brisk tone said: 'Take this book in your right hand and say after me□.□.□.□' I held the book and repeated everything the officer said word for word. He seemed to be an impatient man and not in a very good mood; maybe having to deal with a stupid civilian first thing on a Monday morning wasn't to his liking. But when he had finished he did manage a 'Good morning and good luck to you.'

'We'll go and get your rations,' said the recruiter. So we hurried across a wide area of tarmac to a group of buildings on the far side.

Two men, whom I could now refer to as civilians, were digging a trench near the edge of the tarmac. They were obviously on nodding terms with the recruiter, one of them remarking: 'Ah, you've got yourself a winner this morning then, a candidate for Caterham, I'll be bound.'

'You're half right. They're at Warley now, not Caterham!' said the recruiter.

But I'm afraid this exchange of information didn't enlighten me much at the time as I went on to collect my first army ration. This transpired to be a very small meat pie and a cheese sandwich in a brown paper bag. I became more doubtful still when I signed a chitty for it and noticed it was classified as the rations for the unexpired portion of the day; I remembered Big Rosie's warning about my next meal. I also received a rail-travel warrant, which allowed me to travel free of charge all the way to Warley, Essex – wherever that was.

After a long, wearisome journey, the train approached the outskirts of London, and now I could see why some of my old navvy friends always called it 'the Smoke'. The place was wreathed in a damp, gloomy grey fog. I wondered how people got around in it. I began to get worried in case I got lost, changing trains at King's Cross. I never liked having to ask strangers for directions, in case I was made to look foolish. I have known myself to go miles out of my way rather than ask. Perhaps the story I'd heard about the experience of Pat's John, a neighbour of ours in the Rock, made me wary.

When John and his friend stepped off the boat in Glasgow, all they had was a slip of paper giving the address of someone they would stay with until they found work. John thought the best way to find the address was to chat up a passer-by and then ask for directions as a sort of by-the-way. He also believed that the best people to ask would be the well-dressed ones: they would be sure to know everywhere. John used the weather as his opening gambit. His first victim was a well-dressed business type, complete with bowler hat and umbrella. 'It's a right day, sor!' said John. But the man sidestepped him and hurried past. 'It's a gran' day, sor!' said John to the next one, but still no response. 'Do ye think it'll keep dry, sor?' he greeted someone else, and was ignored again. Being now convinced that no one wanted to chat to him, John scratched his head, turned to his friend and said: 'Begod, they're all in a big hurry the day!'

Luckily, as things turned out, I had no such problems. I was waiting while the ticket collector scrutinised my travel warrant and punched a hole in it. Then I heard a voice say, 'Ah, Mr Devlin!'

'Good Lord,' I thought, 'I've only put my foot in the place and someone knows my name already. These Londoners must be a sharp lot.'

A tall, well-dressed man stepped forward, offering a firm handshake. 'You're on your way to the Guards depot, I believe,' he said. He told me he was a representative of some branch of the army that I didn't catch; then he showed me a badge at the back of his lapel, which I presumed was his authority. 'You've got some time to wait for your next train,' he said, adding, 'I expect you wouldn't say no to a cup of tea and a bite to eat.' I certainly didn't, and thanked the man very much. We went down a long flight of steps from the station and out into the foggy street. People seemed to be hurrying and scurrying in all directions, no doubt trying to get home before the fog got worse. We managed to cross the street in two stages, first from the kerb to an island in the middle of the road, then, by dodging between a bus and a taxi, we finally scrambled to safety. The traffic was crawling at a snail's pace; I wondered how it moved at all without bumping into whatever was in front.

'Take a seat,' the man said as he made his way to the counter of a café. He joined me again in no time, balancing two cups of tea. He went back to the counter for the rest of the order: sausages, mashed potatoes and a slice of bread. I noticed he didn't get anything for himself. 'That will keep you going for a little while longer,' he said as he sat down. He struck me as a man who had been ill and was possibly recuperating. He had a very pale countenance and an anxious little cough, no doubt aggravated by the fog. He asked me what I'd been doing and where, and then went on to explain how different my life was going to be from now on, once I'd completed my training. All I had to do was what I was told and I would soon get the hang of it. The training period was only six months, so I could look forward to being stationed in London by the following May and to participating in the life of the great city. He was quite sure I would never want to go back to navvying again.

With my sausages and mash securely tucked away, I was ready to face any terror the future had in store for me. We went back to the station again and found the train for Warley. The man gave me full directions to the Depot for when I got to the end of the train journey. We shook hands again and he wished me good luck as the train pulled away into the murky gloom. I was glad to have met the man; apart from the sausages and mash, he saved me a lot of anxiety about getting lost. I learned later that the welcome for new arrivals to London did have an ulterior motive. It seemed that many young men were using the army's rail warrant to get to London, where they disappeared without trace; the little bit of courier service I'd just had was an attempt to overcome the problem. But in any event, I never plagued myself with any thoughts about reneging on my contract: I considered it to be equally as binding as any I had made on the Diamond of Derry a few years before. 'In for a penny, in for a pound' was my attitude.

So, come hell or high water, I was going to stick to my side of the bargain.

The fog seemed to be thicker than ever when I got off the train at Warley and cautiously tried to find my bearings. I felt as if I was the only one abroad as I made my way along the street.

Then I heard footsteps approaching and a very tall soldier loomed up out of the fog. 'Can you tell me where the Guards depot is?' I asked.

'You're nearly there. About another 200 yards along on this side,' said the soldier as he disappeared into the fog again.

There was no mistaking the main gate: a soldier stood in a doorway just inside. 'New arrival?' he queried, as he ushered me into a dimly lit room, where another soldier with stripes on his arm greeted me in a most uncivil manner: 'You took yer time getting here! Wha's yer name?' He looked bleary-eyed, as if my arrival had woken him up from a doze. He scribbled a few particulars on a slip of paper and said to the other soldier, 'Take "it" to the receiving room!'

I was taken to the receiving room. 'Another one for you!' said the soldier, addressing the occupants of the room in general – about a dozen young men all in civilian clothes. Some were stretched out on iron cots; others sat round a fireplace without a fire.

'Only one?' queried one occupant.

'Christ, it'll be bloody Christmas before we get a squad at this rate,' said another one.

'I shan't be here come bloody Christmas, a'll tell tha,' remarked some one else.

'You'll have to wait till "Guts-ache" gets back. He'll tell you which bed to have. He's only gone for a pint,' someone advised.

About a dozen beds appeared ready for occupation; the remainder, spaced at intervals round the room, looked as if they could be used as chairs. Not knowing the significance of it all, I would wait until shown how chairs became beds and vice versa. Suddenly the door burst open and a tall soldier entered; he wore a grey-blue overcoat on top of a khaki uniform. His hat had a band of Scots tartan round it and a large badge in the centre, the peak of his cap carrying a strip of glistening brass. He looked fierce. This must be the one they called 'Guts-ache', I thought.

'Got another one since you've been gone,' someone told him.

'Right! Show him how to make his bed down,' the soldier ordered.

'Nothing to it,' said a chap as he grabbed the iron chair and, giving it a little shake, extended it to its full length, so that in a jiffy the chair became a bed. The mattress was in three separate sections, called biscuits; with three blankets and a bolster, that was the bed. Meanwhile, I was watching the soldier-in-charge hanging up his overcoat. He seemed to be performing a kind of ritual. First of all, he laid the coat on his bed and fastened all the buttons; then the belt, which was in two halves at the back, was brought to the front and fastened by one button. He hung the coat on a peg behind his bed and proceeded to pat and stroke it until all the creases and wrinkles had disappeared. I noticed he had sheets on his bed – perhaps one of the perks that went with his job. He looked like a man who had earned any fringe benefits that might be going. He was an 'old soldier' in every sense of the term: bald-headed and with two rows of medal ribbons to prove that much of his service had been of the active kind.

22

IRIS

Paddy Devlin spent three years in the peacetime army and saw service as part of the King's Guard at St James's Palace, as an army fireman and as a rival to the Yeoman Warders at the Tower of London. He also caused an amount of consternation when he sent his civilian clothes home in a parcel without an explanatory note! Back in Civvy Street, he eventually found a job as a maintenance man in a nursing home in Harley Street.

I settled down to my new job rather well, in spite of being the odd man out; at least, there were no complaints so far. Now I had time to cast around for something offering a little more security. The Guards Brigade always had a reputation for being in good standing with the police, and considerable numbers of ex-guardsmen were recruited to the force. But at that time, as in all other public-service departments, recruitment had come to a standstill. Nevertheless, I kept trying. The replies I received were polite, brief and to the point: 'Sorry, no vacancies at present.' On one occasion, however, I thought my luck had changed, on receiving an application form which I was asked to complete and present to the local police station. There, under the watchful eye of an inspector, I was set an exam paper. For all that, the end result was the same: 'Thank you for your application. Sorry, there are no vacancies at present but your name has been added to our waiting list⬚.⬚.⬚.'

'Hi,' I said to myself one day, 'if you're so keen on the police force, why don't you try your own country?' After a little research, however, I had to admit that the difficulties of gaining entry were insurmountable. Firstly, I wasn't sure if British Army reservists were eligible; secondly, a working knowledge of Gaelic was necessary for entry to the Civic Guard. The most important prerequisite of all was knowing the right people. In those days, the job was very much one of patronage: unless you were on nodding terms with your local politician, your application wasn't likely to attract much attention. So, not having sufficient back-up, I had to abandon the idea.

But just a minute, I thought, there are two police forces in Ireland. Why not try the other one? So, without thinking that I might be considered as very naive or a political innocent abroad, I wrote to the Royal Ulster Constabulary. Weeks passed and I had almost forgotten the application when, much to my surprise, I received an application form, which I duly filled in and returned. It wasn't until two years later, when I was home on a visit, that my brother James gave me a verbatim account of what followed.

One day a friend of ours who worked in Derry had a visitor at his place of work. The visitor turned out to be a policeman in civilian clothes. 'Do you know a family named Devlin down your way?' the policeman asked.

'Aye, I do rightly,' our friend replied.

'Who's the head of it?' was the next question.

'That would be James the eldest,' said our friend.

'Next time you see him, will you give him a message? Tell him the next time he's in Derry to call at the police station: the boss would like a word. It's nothing urgent,' said the policeman, as he departed.

Our friend wasn't taking chances, so he came straight to Sarida that night to deliver the message. Both he and James believed that anything involving the police meant trouble of some kind, so James was on the first bus to Derry next morning. The officer at the police station – a pleasant enough man, by all accounts – offered James a seat and, after exchanging the customary remarks on the weather, began his enquiry.

'You have a brother in England, Mr Devlin?'

James, expecting the worst, said, 'Yes.'

'Do you hear from him often?' the officer asked.

'Now and then,' said James.

'Did you know he had applied for a job on the force here?'

James said it was the first he'd heard of it.

'Well, he has, and I've his application form right here in front of me,' said the officer, stabbing a bundle of papers on his desk with his forefinger.

James, not sure whether it was good news or not but aware at least that it wasn't trouble, waited while the officer rose to gaze out of the window for a moment before continuing. 'My next question might appear unnecessary, Mr Devlin, since I know the answer already, but I must be absolutely sure. Where does he go on Sundays?'

With that question out of the way, the officer went on to explain just what the situation was. In a few weeks' time he would be retiring, after thirty years' service, so he had no qualms about telling James how things stood. 'The regulations as they stand at the moment,' he went on, 'allow us to recruit 5 per cent from the Catholic population, but in practice we don't recruit any at all. I want to be fair to your brother without putting it in writing: as things stand at the moment, he would be wasting his time and mine by pursuing his application any further. It's no consolation, I know,' the officer continued, 'but when we do recruit, if your brother's application is anything to go by, he's the sort of young fella we're looking for.' Taken in isolation, this was just a trivial incident – a non-event, you might say. Yet it illustrates how the official policy of sectarianism was pursued. This is how the seeds of dissension are sown: small wonder that Northern Ireland reaped the whirlwind of violence which erupted in the late sixties and continued through the seventies and on into the eighties.

I was walking along the Edgware Road one evening, minding my own business and intending to catch one of Charley Burns's little lectures, when something special on the other side of the road attracted my attention. I spotted a marvellous pair of legs whose owner was idly gazing into a shop window. Always a keen leg man, I thought these worthy of closer inspection, so I crossed over. I was pleasantly surprised to find that, as well as the legs, the superstructure was equally appealing. I found it very difficult to strike up a conversation with a complete stranger without appearing too bold, and I felt a bit ridiculous gazing into a shop window when I realised it was a women's clothes shop. Somehow, I felt that the smart-alec kind of introduction as seen on American films like 'Hi ya, baby?' wouldn't be appropriate on this occasion. We just sidled a little closer to each other until we had to say 'Hello.' So began a long-standing relationship between Paddy Devlin from Donegal and the lovely Iris Howes from Wymondham, Norfolk.

Iris was in domestic service somewhere around Regent's Park Terrace, which in those days was a high-class residential area – seats of the mighty. We sauntered along in that direction, forgetting all about time, until we were abruptly reminded of it by a grand lady waiting on the doorstep: Iris's mistress. She was dressed in all her evening finery, much bejewelled, with long white gloves reaching to her elbows, and a cigarette fixed in an ivory holder. Ignoring me completely, she said, 'Howes! Do you realise what the time is?'

'Yes, madam,' Iris replied, glancing at her watch. 'It's five past ten.'

'You're five minutes late,' madam retorted. 'Go indoors at once.'

Iris whispered 'Goodnight' to me and disappeared down a dark stairway to the basement below. Just then, a big limousine drew near the kerb, stopping where madam was waiting, and a uniformed chauffeur got out and opened the car door. After madam was comfortable in the back seat, the limousine glided away towards the West End.

The next time I saw Iris, she informed me that she was

on the lookout for a new job, because the day after her ticking-off she had given in her notice. 'But why, Howes, why?' madam wanted to know.

'Because I don't like being made a fool of in front of my friends,' Iris replied.

'Ridiculous, Howes! And so silly,' said madam.

Jobs in domestic service were easy to come by at the time; the going rate was ten shillings per week, but paid monthly it probably seemed like more. Iris preferred kitchen work that was considered to be the lowest form of human life in the domestic-service world. She had no desire to blossom forth as a head parlourmaid: her ambition was to become a qualified cook. Although she never finished her apprenticeship, as far as the family and I are concerned she qualified as a first-class cook with honours.

When she and I used to compare notes about our early days, it was remarkable how we moved along parallel lines, particularly when it came to the poverty stakes. While she didn't have to endure the drudgery and loneliness of being hired out for six-month periods, her first job on leaving school was four miles from home, as a general maid in a farmhouse. She laboured from dawn to dusk for the princely sum of four shillings per week. When her half day came round, she would trudge home across the fields. These visits were prolonged to the last possible moment; then her father, after a hard day in the local gravel pits would escort her back to the farm. She still recalls those cold winter nights trudging across the frozen fields with her father, who would wait in the farmyard until he saw the glow from Iris's little candle up in the attic.

'Are you all right now, gel?' he would ask.

'I'm all right now, dad. Goodnight,' Iris would reply. Then she would wait until the sound of his hobnailed boots faded away in the frosty silence.

There was little excitement for a fourteen-year-old who had to work all the hours that God sent in an isolated farmhouse. Eventually Iris began thinking about some means of opting out; if an opportunity didn't present itself soon, she would have to make one. It was now midsummer, and one Sunday morning she was down on her knees scrubbing the larder floor. Her mistress appeared on the scene and demanded to know why the larder was being scrubbed on a Sunday, when it should have been done on Saturday.

Whatever reason Iris gave, it didn't sound convincing enough for madam, who retorted: 'If you spent less time leaning out of the window, waving to the boys on the farm, you would get your work done on the day it should be done.'

The air became very tense as Iris thought about dropping the wet floor-cloth (called a 'dwile' in Norfolk) on madam's feet. But she had second thoughts and politely said, 'Please move out of my way.'

'Indeed I will not!' said madam. 'This is my house. Move out of *your* way indeed!' she continued. There was a large preserving pan standing in the corner, full to the brim with eggs. Iris grabbed as many as she could lay hands on and pelted her mistress all the way up the stairs. Covered in dripping yolk, madam screamed for her husband, who, as far as Iris remembers, never answered his wife's distress call. Iris, having burned her boats, dashed to the attic and stuffed her belongings into her old suitcase. She had an accumulation of old coats from her visits home during the winter: she put on as many as she could get on, and the rest she draped round her shoulders. Thus attired and carrying the old suitcase, she set out across the fields for the last time, heading for home. It was a scorching hot day in June and poor Iris was deadbeat by the time she got to Wymondham.

A neighbour, seeing this strange apparition coming along the road, came out to investigate. 'Is that you, Iris?' she enquired as she peered under the coats. This kind neighbour lent her an old pram, and so, with all the old coats aboard and the old suitcase perched on top, Iris continued her journey, somewhat apprehensive about how her mother would react to this kind of homecoming. The loss of four shillings per week could have a catastrophic impact on the family budget in those days. Much to Iris's surprise, her mother, on hearing the story, was more than sympathetic: while the loss of four shillings per week was no joke, the knowledge that her youngest daughter was 'a chip off the old block' made up for it. Later on, having raised her sights a little, Iris joined her elder sister in London, who was now an experienced house parlourmaid and doing well. The partnership wasn't a happy one: Iris resented being chaperoned. She was a big girl now and could take care of herself. So she went freelancing until we bumped into each other in the Edgware Road.

I suppose, by today's standards, two years would be considered a long period of courtship, but in those times no job prospects and lack of security were the cause of many postponed marriages. In the end Iris and I decided to make a break for it and take our chances, in spite of the grim prevailing conditions. We probably still hold the record for the quietest wedding ever celebrated at the famous St James's, Spanish Place, W1. Those present were Iris, myself, the priest and his verger. Poor Iris shed a few tears during the ceremony: she was lonely and, if the truth were known, the pair of us were wondering if we were doing the right thing.

The priest tried to cheer us up a little by remarking to the verger, 'This is the kind of wedding we like, don't we, Mr Mahoney?'

'Aye, we do that,' Mr. Mahoney replied. 'No fuss, no bother and no sweeping-up afterwards.'

They shook hands with us and wished us good luck.

So it was to hell with poverty, as we hailed our first ever London taxi and headed for our first home, a furnished room in Hethpool Street, Paddington. We celebrated the occasion with a high tea which included a great slab of lemon cake, to which both of us were a bit partial. In the evening we went to the West End and from the most expensive seats in a very posh cinema we watched the great screen epic of that time, *King Kong*. Glued to our seats, we watched Fay Wray being dangled from the roof of the Empire State Building by the notorious monster.

23

LIVING ON LOVE

As I had left my job of my own accord, I wasn't eligible to draw unemployment pay for a period of six weeks. Meanwhile, I took the precaution of re-registering with the National Ex-Serviceman's Association and the Guards Employment Society, just in case. What meagre savings we had we left in a very large suitcase on top of the wardrobe; every time shopping was required, we just went to the suitcase. Our savings soon dwindled; even so, Iris insisted on our having only best English steak, at one and six a pound. We spotted an advert in one of the Sunday papers which simply said 'Earn More Money!' But you had to speculate before you could accumulate, by sending five pounds to a firm in Leicester. In return we would receive a tool kit, two sacks of material and a set of instructions. Providing we followed the instructions to the letter and worked hard, we could produce leather mats, for which the firm in Leicester would pay us twenty-five pounds.

Both Iris and I agreed that the sooner we got cracking and became self-employed the sooner the twenty-five-pound cheques would commence rolling in. We took another fiver from the suitcase and despatched it to Leicester. The leather material arrived within a few days and proved to be just scraps of leather – waste material from some shoe factory. Iris and I got to work immediately: we studied the instructions carefully before attaching the little cutting machine to the corner of the table, which we intended to use as our workbench. But every time we pulled the handle of the little machine it reacted with a loud bump, so it wasn't long before the landlady appeared, wanting to know what was causing all the noise. She couldn't possibly allow that awful noise in the house, and rightly so, but in our anxiety to get hold of our first twenty-five-pound cheque, we overlooked the disturbance we were causing.

The only way to proceed now was to find a proper workshop, so we searched around until we found a derelict basement in Praed Street. The occupants on the ground floor said the basement belonged to them and we could rent it for five shillings per week. Quite a number of steps on the wooden stairway were missing, there was no light and the door was gone, so to get to our workshop we had to proceed with caution. Sufficient daylight filtered through from street-level to allow us to work on a little bench we rigged up near a broken window. We laboured hard through all the hours daylight would permit, Iris threading the little pieces of leather on the wire frames as they came off my cutting machine. We were anxious to get the first consignment completed. The reason wasn't hard to seek: every time we went to get a pound from the suitcase, we could tell how much was left without counting it. So we set ourselves a deadline: the week prior to the August bank holiday. That way, we reckoned we would have our twenty-five-pound cheque in time to spend the bank holiday in comfort. At last our leather mats were finished and ready for despatch. I borrowed a street totter's barrow for half a crown, loaded the mats and trundled them all the way to Kings Cross Station goods depot.

All we had to do now was sit back and wait for the postman, but after an anxious week, Friday came and there was still no cheque. There was nothing unusual about the horse-drawn railway cart as it came along the street until it stopped at our landlady's door.

'You're wanted, Mr Devlin,' the landlady shouted up the stairs.

'I've got some leather material for you,' the railway-man said.

That's a good sign, I thought: they want another con-signment made up. Sadly, it wasn't like that at all: an accompanying note said the mats were not acceptable because they weren't made to the correct specifications. However, the firm at Leicester said it would have no objection to our disposing of the mats if we wished. The railwayman said there was a freight charge of seven and six to be collected but I refused to pay, so he simply said, 'Ah, well, I'll just take the stuff back to the depot.' That was the last we saw or heard of our leather mats. We realised then, of course, that we had been conned: the mats were simply a gimmick to sell the little leather-cutting machine which was worth no more than a pound. Iris and I were just another couple of mugs from whom the firm in Leicester had made another four pounds' profit.

Neither of us was feeling on top of the world as we mingled with the throngs of people in Hyde Park on bank holiday Monday. That was, until I got a terrific whack between the shoulder blades and a voice behind said: 'Christ, if it isn't my old mate Joe Devlin!' Such a familiar greeting could only come from my old friend Skipper; he and his wife were standing behind us. They were living in Fulham, where Skipper had a temporary job on the local council. When we told them about our problems, they insisted that we moved to Fulham immediately: their next-door neighbour had a spare room to let. Next day we became residents of Fulham.

When I went to sign on at the local labour exchange, I discovered that I was now entitled to unemployment benefit, so at least we would have a roof over our heads, for a week or two anyway. This was something to be thankful for, as Iris had proudly informed me that our first child was well on its way. There was no work, of course, but I knew Skipper was keeping a sharp lookout for me. The queues at the labour exchange seemed to get longer every day, with many people looking desperate. After a week or two, the blow fell. 'No more benefit,' the clerk told me. 'See the manager,' he added.

I joined the most desperate queue of all: a long line of men in the same predicament as myself, waiting for the manager's attention. 'What do I do now?' I asked when he told me I was out of benefit.

'Go to the Assistance Board,' he told me, as he handed me a card authorising Iris and me to attend at the offices of the Assistance Board the following Thursday.

This office was situated in very appropriate surroundings: it was part of an old workhouse building attached to Fulham Hospital. A wee slip of a girl handed me a lengthy questionnaire which had to be completed on the spot before we joined a large number of others occupying wooden benches in the corridor, waiting for their names to be called out. When our turn came, Iris and I found ourselves in a small room, facing a lady and gentleman sitting behind a raised desk. They looked a formidable pair. The lady was dressed in a very sober-looking tweed suit; the pince-nez balanced on the end of her nose was secured by a silver chain round her neck. Perusing my questionnaire, from time to time she would drop the pince-nez, which seemed to bounce on her ample bosom as she discussed some point with her colleague. He in turn was watching us and weighing us up very closely; now and again he would nod at whatever remarks the lady was making. His wing collar and the very fancy-looking pin in his black tie fascinated me. I found myself trying to conjure up nicknames for the two of them: the best I could do was Mr Wing Nut and Mrs Tweedy.

Although Mrs Tweedy was obviously the boss, she leaned heavily on Mr Wing Nut for advice. There were many 'um's and 'ah's and 'yes's as they conferred with each other almost in whispers. At last Mrs Tweedy opened up the proceedings with: 'Well now, Mr Devlin, how long have you been out of work? What was your last job? How long were you in it? And before that?' Rustling my questionnaire between her finger and thumb, she continued: 'You say you are paying ten shillings per week rent. Couldn't you find something a little less expensive? Have you thought about the Industrial Dwellings for the Poor, for example?'

At this point, Mr Wing Nut intervened with a little cough and whispered something to her ladyship.

'Um. Ah. Yes, of course,' she replied. He had most probably advised her that the Industrial Dwellings let only unfurnished accommodation. Then she changed her tack. 'Mrs Devlin, you were in domestic service before you married.'

Mr Wing Nut gave another little cough and they had another little whisper.

'Um. Ah. I see,' said her ladyship. If she was about to suggest that Iris should take up domestic service again, Mr Wing Nut, being an observant man, no doubt drew attention to Iris's obvious condition. Madam somehow hadn't noticed. 'You will keep looking for work, won't you, Mr Devlin?' asked madam. 'You will think about that rent: every shilling counts these days, you know.'

The interview seemed to have finished; Iris and I just sat waiting for the verdict. Our inquisitors were now engaged in whispered conversation. Mrs Tweedy scribbled something in an account book, tore the page out and handed it to me. 'Take this along to the cashier,' she said. 'It isn't much but it will tide you over for a day or two. I hope you find a job soon. Good morning.' The cashier in his little cubbyhole snatched the chitty from me and belaboured it so hard with a date-stamp I thought his desk would fall apart. Taking a pound from his cash box, he flicked it at me. Before I had time to catch it, it fluttered down to the corridor floor. Had the window been wide enough, I would have grabbed him through it by his scrawny neck, choked him and made him pick the note up. I couldn't help feeling there was a grain of truth in the old saying: 'There is no official more insufferable than a petty official from a peasant background.' All those little Hitlers inside their little cubicles in labour exchanges and the like seemed to be hand-picked for the job. They seemed to have a special capacity for rudeness and unsympathetic behaviour towards those unfortunates who had to seek their help.

24

LANDSCAPE GARDENER, FILM EXTRA OR LINESMAN?

The next time I went to sign on, I was told: 'See the manager.' What, again? I thought. There was no queue this time; he had a green card with a note attached waiting for me. 'This firm has a vacancy for a temporary labourer. Want to give it a try?'

'Yes please,' said I, and away I went as happy as a sandboy to the address of a firm of agricultural and landscape gardeners just off Kensington High Street. It was a one-man firm, run by an ex-army major. He found the contracts; his wife was the architect and did all the drawings and paperwork. There were two permanent employees, experts in stonewalling, crazy paving, turf-laying and the like. There was work for a labourer for two or three weeks at least; the pay was a shilling an hour, and there was also an opportunity to learn all the skills associated with landscape gardening. I jumped at the opportunity. So pleased was I to be earning once again, I ran most of the way back to our room to give Iris the glad tidings. She was out somewhere, so I left a message: I scribbled 'Got a job!' on a mirror with a piece of candle. Iris still recalls the message; it made one of her happiest days.

Apart from finding the rent, we now had to give serious thought to the accommodation problems. Landladies with rooms to let made no bones about the fact that they didn't want expectant mothers as tenants. Finding unfurnished accommodation was simple enough; the problem was how to obtain furniture without cash. Although credit terms were available at all furniture stores, a cash deposit was necessary. So, once again, it was our old friend Skipper who came to the rescue by introducing us to the manager of a local furniture store. The manager agreed to waive the cash-deposit formality and provide us with enough furniture and lino for two rooms, in return for my Army Reserve paybook. No doubt this was a highly illegal breach of army regulations, but needs must! Providing we could find the rent, we could now enjoy security of tenure in unfurnished accommodation.

There was no housing shortage in Fulham in those days. Housing agents could supply a list of at least thirty vacant properties – houses, flats and so on – any day. They would give you a list and a bunch of keys, and it was merely a case of looking around and helping yourself. Iris and I used to wander round at our leisure, looking for some quiet side street. But this could be deceptive: many streets looked nice and peaceful during the day until the children came home from school, and then it was complete bedlam. Most of the vacant flats were freshly decorated, ready for new tenants, but Iris and I, being a couple of greenhorns at the game, didn't realise there were other problems to contend with. The local cockneys would have the flat earmarked for a relation or friend and would rather have someone they knew in the house than strangers. I'm sure this was definitely the case the morning I went along to look over an empty flat in a very nice, sedate-looking side street.

As I was opening the front door, I could see an elderly lady watching me from the basement. After having a good look at the flat and deciding it was just what we wanted, I heard a voice from behind me say: 'Shouldn't have it, mate!'

I turned round to face the old lady from the basement. She was puffing a fag end and still wheezing from her effort to climb the stairs. 'It looks very nice,' I said. 'Just what the wife and I were looking for.'

'Naw, steam-tugs, mate,' said the lady.

'Oh!' said I, raising myself on tiptoe to look out the window. 'I didn't know it was that close to the river.'

'Naw,' said the lady, 'I mean the ones that crawl up and darn the wall, not the ones that sail up and darn the river. Ye silly bleeder. Bugs!'

Enough said, I thought, and took the lady's advice at face value and left. She no doubt was pleased at getting rid of another stranger.

In the end we settled for two rooms on the top floor of a privately owned house near Fulham Cross. The landlady was a kindly soul, the motherly type: she took to us as if we were her own family, and we got along famously. I don't think her husband felt the same way about us; possibly he didn't like having to share his home with strangers. Later on, when our first child, Patricia, arrived and he had to squeeze past a pram in the hall, maybe he began to think the house wasn't his any more.

My landscape-gardening career tended to be a bit intermittent. Some contracts lasted four or five weeks; then there would be a gap of a week or two before the next one came along. But I liked the work while it lasted and gradually I built up a pleasant form of camaraderie with my workmates. Life wasn't too desperate at all. I decided it wouldn't be a bad idea to become a bit more mobile, travel further, save bus fares and possibly pick up another little job to tide me over between the land-scaping contracts. A firm in Sheffield supplied the answer by offering a brand new bicycle for ten shillings down and threepence a week until the sum of three pounds ten was paid. In due course I became the owner of my first brand-new bike. And a sturdy machine it was, with a twenty-six-inch frame and very upright handlebars, causing one of my workmates to remark: 'You look like an old Irish priest, riding about on that thing.' True, it bore no comparison to my old boss's streamlined road-racer in those halcyon days back in the County Derry, but I was just as proud of it as I had been of that bike.

During this period, the silence from the National Ex-Servicemen's Association and the Guards' Employment Society was almost deafening. I was beginning to think I had been forgotten about altogether, until like a bolt from the blue a card arrived from each of them by the same post. Things were taking a turn for the better all of a sudden. The Guards' Employment Society told me to report to a firm of film-wardrobe outfitters in Wardour Street, Soho, before proceeding to somewhere near Park

Royal to do crowd work in the great historical film *The Iron Duke.* Here was excitement and adventure being handed to me on a plate, and the money was good too: a guinea a day. But most important of all, my favourite film actor, George Arliss, was playing the leading role. In the excitement, I hadn't even glanced at the card from the National Ex-Servicemen's Association; when I did, I was brought back to earth immediately. The card informed me that the GPO Engineering Department was offering temporary employment to a small number of ex-servicemen. So, as someone once said, 'There is a tide in the affairs of all men⬚.⬚.⬚.⬚'

With some reluctance, I decided the great George Arliss would have to portray the famous Iron Duke without me: my own Waterloo was staring me in the face. My film career might not last more than three or four days, while the GPO offer, albeit temporary, sounded much more substantial. I decided to grab it. I was about to mount my trusty bike and head for Victoria Street when I received a clout on the ear from one of the landlady's slippers, which she had thrown at me. 'That's for good luck,' she shouted after me.

An interview with a GPO official a few days later seemed no more than a formality. I was to report to Kensington Telephone Exchange on the following Monday morning, to commence duties as a labourer on a starting pay of two pounds six and eightpence per week. Telephone engineering was a new line of country for me entirely. I had no idea what to expect as I mingled with a crowd of strangers as they signed in for their day's work. There were two other new entrants besides myself, and when the foreman, accompanied by another man, came to look us over, he asked: 'Any of you got a bike?'

'Yes,' said I promptly.

'He's yours then, Ernie,' said the foreman.

'Better get the tools then,' said Ernie, who disappeared into the building and came back with a Gladstone bag, which I found quite heavy as I balanced it on my handlebars.

Hope it doesn't scratch my paintwork, I thought. Ernie strapped a stout leather case to his back; this, I later discovered, was a portable telephone. He led the way as we pedalled round the side streets of Chelsea until we came to an establishment where many more bikes were leaning against the wall. It was the local tea shop. The shop was almost full to capacity. Mugs of tea and slices of toast and dripping were being served up by a stout, comely lady whom everyone called Nell. Nell's was obviously the place where all the local notables from the telephone exchange, the gas company and the electricity department gathered for an early-morning mug of tea before commencing their day's duties. Ernie and I had a good chat over our mugs of tea and a fag; he explained that he was an emergency-faults troubleshooter. He was on what he called 'straights' that week, meaning normal working hours of 7.30 am to 5 pm, rotating with his opposite number, whose duty covered the period 10 am to 8 pm. Fire, police, ambulance and some doctors' lines had priority for emergency treatment. Even when Ernie and his partner were off duty, they were on emergency standby and could be called out at any hour. Ernie wanted my address so that he could give me a shout if required, providing I had no objection – which I hadn't, since all extra duties were at overtime rates.

But there was more to it than just carrying the tools around for Ernie. I was expected to make myself useful in many other ways as well. Trying to identify the right cable from among the mass of others that ran in all directions under London's pavements required a sharp eye. When the identification marks were missing, as they very often were, I would try to move the cables by pulling them, until Ernie identified the one he wanted. He showed me how to remove those box covers, seen on the pavement and marked 'GPO Telephones', without causing a hernia. When one day he told me I'd 'got the right knack', he laughed like hell when I said: 'Aye, and the left one helps as well.'

Invariably, near knocking-off time, another emergency would be reported and Ernie and I would pedal off again to try to find the trouble. The extra duty or overtime would average three or four hours a week and Iris got into the habit of not expecting me home until I got there. The extra money on pay day, however, made up for some of the inconvenience. Now and again Ernie and I and the other emergency team would get involved with what was called a 'big 'un' – a cable breakdown. There were occasions when he would wake me up at two or three in the morning and tell me where to find him, once I had woken up properly after a cup of scalding tea and a fag. I can recall spending the whole of an Easter bank holiday down a manhole in Brompton Road on one of Ernie's breakdowns, and the following day taking seven pounds home to a delighted Iris.

Although a non-technical person, I soon found myself becoming very interested in the work of a telephone linesman. I was fascinated by the ease with which Ernie could recognise the wires he wanted from the mass of little wires in a cable. In the end I decided to find out for myself by asking Ernie lots of questions and jotting the answers down in my little notebook. Later I discovered that the Post Office could supply a wide range of technical pamphlets on demand to anyone who was interested. I always carried one around with me and any spare moment I had on the job I spent studying it. I had a feeling that poor old Ernie was getting fed up with all my questioning, especially when one day he retorted: 'Why don't you go to evening classes?' Until then I wasn't aware that such a facility existed but all I had to do, apparently, was make a request through the usual channels. In return I had to agree to attend the nearest polytechnic, in my case Battersea, for two evenings per week from September to March, all for free to the student. But there were other important issues to be considered. It meant I wouldn't be available for any overtime that might be going on those two nights and it would be at least 10 pm before I got home on each occasion. Either way, sacrifices had to be made: loss of much-needed extra money had to be balanced with the possible gain of technical merit which might or might not pay off later. It was like buying 'a pig in a poke'.

25

ON THE BEACH

Paddy did eventually get enough certificates, as his new gaffer, Tich, said, to 'paper the bedroom': qualifications which stood him in good stead later. As a reservist, he was called up almost immediately when war came in 1939, and June 1940 found him, like so many others, stranded on the beach at Dunkirk.

My mate and I sat down behind our barricade to ponder the imponderable. Although we had anticipated a situation such as this, now that we were confronted with the reality, we couldn't take it all in. When we realised that we were expendable, we felt very vulnerable indeed. Our only hope was that the Germans wouldn't move in before daylight. The atmosphere of Furnes was now that of an eerie ghost town. About midnight, the weather changed and quite a strong breeze blew up. We sat listening to shutters and doors squeaking and banging in the darkness; an old tin can of some kind, caught in the breeze, trundled along the pavement, as if someone was idly kicking it. This was going to be the longest two hours and twenty-five minutes in the whole campaign. We kept looking at our watches, shaking them and holding them to our ears to make sure they hadn't stopped. We each lit another Craven A, checked our battle order, tightened our gas masks and put our steel helmets on straight. If we'd had any polish, we would have polished our boots: no task was too trivial as long as it made time pass.

At 1.25 am exactly, we grabbed the Bren and the magazines and crept to the door. From there we could make out the silhouette of the church at the bottom of the town. Almost on tiptoe, we crept past the piles of fallen masonry in the street until we reached the church entrance. A quiet voice in the darkness said, 'Over here!' We recognised it as belonging to one of our drill sergeants. The rest of the holding party crept in pairs after us. When everyone was accounted for, the sergeant said: 'Right, tear those blankets up in strips and wrap them round your boots, so that you don't make a noise on the cobbles when you get outside.' So, in the pitch darkness of the church, we tugged and pulled at the blankets, reducing them to strips of all shapes and sizes. We had to dive for the floor when a shell struck the other end of the church. From the noise of falling masonry, it sounded as if the spire had been demolished. The next shell came a little closer, landing in the centre of the building. I was stretched out on the floor close to a main pillar near the entrance. A lump of masonry crashed on top of me. It was a large crucifix; fortunately for me, it was of a light plaster material. Had it been the traditional wooden cross, I might not have got away so lightly.

When the shelling ceased, with our boots wrapped in

bits of army blanket, we ventured forth, a little wobbly, on the last lap of our journey to the beach at La Panne. Creeping along on flannel feet, we soon ran into all kinds of obstacles, the worst being festoons of demasted telephone wires; we lost a lot of time disentangling ourselves from the stuff. Away ahead of us we could see what looked like a huge bonfire, into which the Germans were pumping a continuous barrage of mortar shells. But, with the canal on one side and a waterlogged marshland on the other, the high cobblestone road was the only way forward. Stopping to disentangle ourselves from the blasted telephone wires, we could hear the pounding of hooves and the neighing and snorting of horses. What sounded like a herd of them seemed to be galloping back and forth in a field alongside the canal, probably panic-stricken by the mortar-fire and the flames up ahead. From what looked like a house on the other side of the canal we could hear a baby screaming – loud screams that gradually faded to faint sobbing, as if the child was trapped somewhere.

Although the idea behind them was good, the strips of blanket weren't successful. One of mine came undone and had to be abandoned; after trying to get along doing a kind of 'dot and carry', I said 'to hell with it' and abandoned the other one as well. The scene where the fire was raging was indescribable. A number of ambulances caught in the mortar-fire were now almost burned out. Bodies of the dead were strewn about everywhere, and there were cries from the injured who had been blown into the marshes. The road was now cut in two as a result of the shelling. How to get across the crater in the pitch dark and keep alive was the main preoccupation.

Someone on the far side who had made it successfully was using his cupped hands as a loud hailer and shouting advice back to us. 'Wait for the fourth one! Count four!' he kept shouting. This was timely advice indeed, because in our previous experience of mortar-fire we noticed that there was a pattern. Apart from deadly accuracy, the bombs seemed to be fired in a series of four. Then there was a slight pause for a second or two: provided you still had your wits about you, there was time to run a few yards and, with luck, get out of harm's way before the next series began. The big snag was the crater: by the time we jumped in and scrambled up the other side, precious seconds would be lost. So we lay on the cobblestones counting and listening for that all-important pause between bombardments. I counted one of a fresh series and gripped my rifle, ready to make a dive on number four. Bomb number two landed in front of me with a blinding crash. The rifle shivered in my hand, sending pins and needles up my arm. A large chunk of white-hot metal lay in front of me. A small white cloud appeared at ground level and, as if framed in its centre, was Iris's face. She was smiling and nodding to me as if she were saying: 'Come on, get going! You're all right!'

I dived for the crater and pulled myself up the other side. Still in a crouched position, I ran forward into the arms of someone, who shouted 'In here!' as he pushed me into a hollow in the sand dunes. It took a while to get my breath back. The smell of petrol and burning rubber from the wrecked ambulances lay thick in the hollow, in spite of the breeze whistling through the marram grass.

The others were talking in whispers and, although it was difficult to see in the dark, I reckoned there were at least twenty sheltering in the hollow. At least a dozen of them belonged to our other two battalions, who like ourselves had been left to hold the fort around Furnes. The man whom I ran into on clearing the crater turned out to be an adjutant from one of the other battalions. He kept returning to the hollow to enquire if we were still all right. We could hear the child crying again. When someone asked if something could be done about that 'Baba', the adjutant said: 'It's being seen too. The nuns are with it.'

Meanwhile, having recovered my composure, I examined my rifle: to my astonishment, I found that the barrel was completely stripped of its woodwork. The muzzle end was bent in a half-'S' shape; it could be hung on a nail and, now that it was the perfect museum piece, I was determined to hang on to it at all costs. The adjutant came back to explain that he wanted us to wait, in case there were others still stranded on the wrong side of the crater. We told him it was unlikely, since we were the holding party and the last to leave Furnes; whereupon he said: 'All right. Fall in in threes.' We stumbled out of the sand dunes onto the cobblestones with a 'Quick march!' We followed the adjutant towards the beach. It was a welcome change to be moving in threes once again. I had a feeling that all wasn't lost yet, at least for a little while. We soon found ourselves up to the ankles in loose sand. At the high-water mark we could just make out a long row of army lorries buried up to the chassis in the sand; it looked as if they had been used as a makeshift pier earlier. Now on the firm wet sand, we marched on towards the water's edge. As we got closer we could make out a long dark shadow between us and the incoming tide. The shadow turned out to be a seemingly endless queue of soldiers. We wheeled round and halted, with our backs to the queue.

The adjutant proceeded to give us another little homily but he had nothing new to add to what we had been told already. In retrospect, however, like everyone else, his feelings of frustration can well be appreciated. There was little reward in marching your men to the edge of the sea and having to say: 'I'm sorry, this is as far as I can take you.' Now it was going to be a case of every man for himself. With the queue appearing to stretch for miles in either direction and with a deadline of less than twenty-four hours to beat, it was a dismal situation indeed.

While the adjutant was talking, a funny little man from the queue tried to amuse the crowd by creating a diversion. He was drunk, of course, and kept staggering round us, taking the rise as he went. But the audience failed to rise to the occasion: it was not a funny situation. Nonetheless, the little man tried his best with remarks like: 'Look at the silly buggers, still trying to be soldiers. They'll be trooping the colour any minute.' The adjutant kept running his stick across his hand and I believe that if the little fellow had got any closer, the adjutant would have swiped him one. However, someone in the queue saved him the bother by shouting: 'Why don't you fuck off?' The would-be comic did just that, staggering away along the beach, humming a little tune.

After reminding us once again about the last transport leaving Dunkirk at midnight, the adjutant wished us good luck, and away he went along the beach. We latched ourselves onto the queue exactly where we had halted, although we were expecting any minute someone to shout: 'How about you lot going to the end of the queue then?' But nobody challenged us.

Surf from the incoming tide was producing a most unusual ground-lighting effect due to phosphorescence; even as we moved about on the wet sand, it stuck to our boots like glow-worms. It would be easy for marauding aircraft to attack the queue, using the glowing surf as a marker. The Luftwaffe, however, seemed not to be in a hurry and were waiting for daylight. Someone behind me became interested in my strange-looking rifle. 'What are you carrying that useless thing around with you for?' he asked. 'Don't be silly,' I replied, 'this is the new Mark 4.' Holding the rifle up in the air, I said: 'Look, it's for shooting round corners.' In normal circumstances, such a silly remark might at least have raised a giggle. On this occasion there wasn't even a titter, which was a bad sign: the army's sense of humour had reached its lowest ebb. This was the first time in history it had been driven into the sea, and even now, as the tide washed over its boots, it refused to believe it. Everyone was looking for a scapegoat: the troops in their own vernacular were saying that some bastard, somewhere, was responsible for this lot.

Meanwhile, the nearest target for such remarks was the RAF. There was no doubt in anyone's mind that German superiority in the air and on the ground made it look as if the RAF was non-existent. This wasn't the case, of course, but soldiers stranded on the beaches of Dunkirk and La Panne would take a lot of convincing that the situation was otherwise. Our party broke up into its original little groups as it joined the queue. Now there were just six of us in one little bunch. There didn't seem to be any movement up ahead at all, and we kept edging sideways towards the dunes as the strength of the tide increased. There was a momentary diversion when a soldier came striding towards us from the dunes. He was talking loudly to himself and kept repeating: 'I can see them. I can see them.' As he elbowed his way through our little group, almost knocking some of us over, everyone shouted: 'Look out, you silly bugger, you're going in the sea!' Taking no notice at all, the man just waded on into the tide. His last 'I can see them' came as bubbles from under his steel helmet as he disappeared under a wave.

Streaks of dawn were beginning to appear above the smoke clouds over Dunkirk as the Luftwaffe took to the air once again. The Messerschmitt overhead was flying so low we had to hang on to our steel helmets for fear of losing them in the slipstream. It turned out to be a dummy run, the pilot no doubt checking his bearings to get the queue in his gunsight ready for the real thing. At the front of the queue he banked over, came round in a wide sweep and started firing away behind us. In panic, most of the queue scattered: those nearest the sea threw themselves in, those nearest the dunes ran for it, while we in the middle had no time to do anything but stay put and lean forward, presenting as small a target as possible. Those who ran for the dunes got caught as tracer bullets ripped into the wet sand, leaving a trail of dead, dying and wounded. Still not satisfied with his handiwork, the sod banked over again and swept round to finish us off.

Then, as if from nowhere, two men appeared on the edge of the dunes firing a Bren gun. Everyone was amazed to see the gunner standing bolt upright and firing from the hip; his mate was crouched behind him, using his back to support the gunner. Somehow they maintained an arc of fire and, because the Messerschmitt was flying low, it had no choice but to fly into a stream of bullets. After firing a couple of bursts, the plane's guns went silent, the engine began to cough and splutter, and we were almost choked by a cloud of black smoke pouring from the tailplane. There was a mad panic when everyone thought the plane was going to crash down on top of us, but it veered to the left and skimmed the sand dunes until it hit the ground with a loud thud. The effect was electrifying: the crowd, who a moment before had been panic-stricken, now burst into loud cheering which would have done justice to a cup final. Then everything went quiet as we waited for the plane to explode. Minutes passed but nothing happened. We watched half a dozen men as they raced towards the dunes. 'Let's get the bastard!' they shouted as they went. It wasn't long before we heard a long, agonising scream coming from the direction of the fallen plane. A little later the men came back and quietly rejoined the queue.

So it was, amid the chaos, that another line or two of military history was created. The two unorthodox Bren-gunners were French officers. As a result of their action, the use of Bren guns as an anti-aircraft weapon was extended to include 'hose-piping'.

It was now full daylight and the queue was settling down again after the panic. Our little group of six went

into a huddle and began to assess the situation, specu-
lating on what was the best thing to do in order to
survive. 'What do you think, Dev? You're the old soldier
– got any theories?' someone asked. But the options were
so limited; it would take more than a theory to improve
matters. There was quite a hazy mist at sea level; when
it broke in places, we could see at least two fairly large
boats anchored well out in deep water. We also caught a
glimpse of a small rowing boat loaded with soldiers being
ferried out from the beach. At least something was
happening, although the queue didn't appear to get any
shorter. We had no choice but to stay put and wait our
turn for the little rowing boat, bearing in mind that the
Luftwaffe might attack in strength at any minute. In any
event, it could only be a matter of hours before we would
be staring down the barrels of the Panzers' 88 mm guns
when they lined up on the dunes for the *coup de grâce.*

26

ALL ABOARD *THE MEDWAY QUEEN*

We toyed with the idea of searching through all the
wreckage on the beach to find something floatable so that
we could put to sea and, with luck, get picked up. Finally,
as a last resort, we could take the adjutant's advice:
shelter in the dunes until evening and then make for
Dunkirk and that last transport to England. We weren't
aware that Dunkirk harbour was already out of action and
that this was why attempts were being made to lift troops
directly off the beach. We finally decided to keep ourselves occupied, so we left our place in the queue and set
off to find out what was happening up front, where the
rowing boat was being loaded. There we found a reasonably well-organised system in operation, albeit one that
was painfully slow.

Standing on an improvised platform with the tide
already washing over his boots was a major of artillery,
supervising the loading of the little rowing boat, which
seemed to have a lone sailor in charge. Sixteen was the
boat's capacity; this we learned because the major was
shouting: 'Sixteen only!' It would seem that in the

scramble, a seventeenth man got on board, hoping the major wouldn't spot him. 'You! That last man. Get off!' the major shouted. The man didn't respond so the major warned him again. 'Get off or I shoot!' Still the bewildered man didn't move, so the major drew his revolver and shot him in the shoulder. On the sand nearby lay a Bren gun, its magazine in position ready for anti-aircraft defence. A tall soldier sprang from the queue, grabbed the gun and was about to point it at the major when two or three other soldiers grabbed him. After a brief wrestle on the wet sand, the would-be assassin was disarmed and led away along the beach. Having witnessed that incident, we were finally convinced there was no future for us in the queue. We went on searching through the old bits of wreckage.

We became so engrossed in our foraging mission that we didn't realise just how far we had wandered from the queue. In fact it now looked as if we had a little bit of beach all to ourselves.

The foraging stopped when one of the lads exclaimed: 'Hang on a minute, there's a rowing boat out there!'

'Where? Where?' the rest of us wanted to know.

'Out there!' he said, pointing a finger towards the misty sea.

'You're imagining it, mate,' someone ventured.

'I'm telling ya I saw a bloody rowing boat out there, na then!'

We all gathered in a huddle and tried to peer under the mist, just in case. 'Bloody mirage, ol' cock, that's what it was. The only boats out there are at the bottom of the briny,' someone dolefully said.

'Aw, please ya bloody sel's then,' said our friend, sounding a little bit narked.

'He's right, you know,' I said, having just spotted a white object bobbing about on the waves before it disappeared in the mist.

'There it is, and there's some bugger in it,' cried our friend enthusiastically, secure in the knowledge that he was right after all.

We all raced into the sea, shouting: 'Hi, there! Over here!' The strong tide soon enveloped us and the water was so bloody cold that it wasn't long before we were all gulping for air. At first we felt quite buoyant, our water-filled trousers acting as a kind of pontoon. When we were thoroughly soaked, however, the situation was reversed; 200 rounds of ammunition, rifles and hand grenades became a bit of a handicap. I began to feel as if I was wearing diver's gear. In a desperate bid to keep our heads above the water, we joined hands to form a human chain: this restored confidence quite a bit, especially to non-swimmers like myself. We must have looked like bobbins on a fishing net to the lone figure in the rowing boat as he loomed up amongst us in the fog.

There was a desperate scramble to get out of the sea, until the boatman shouted: 'Hang on, hang on! Take it steady or you'll have her over!' The civilian voice of common sense quietened us down, and some held the boat steady while the others scrambled aboard. Being last as usual, I almost panicked, thinking I wasn't going to make it. I was trying to board at the wrong time, when the boat was on the crest of a wave, instead of waiting for the slough. My greatest impediment was the bloody gas mask: I just couldn't get it over the lip of the boat. Then, in one desperate attempt and with the help of one or two of my mates, I landed on my head in the bottom of the boat.

'All right,' said the boatman, 'anyone done any rowing afore? 'Cos if not, now's yer chance to larn.' Being nearest to a rowlock, I grabbed an oar. However, from the word go it was clear that neither I nor the bloke on the other oar had the foggiest idea about rowing. The boat insisted on going round in a circle, until the boatman intervened. 'Hang on, hang on,' he repeated. 'Let's get her pointed in the right direction. We don't want to go back to the bloody beach, do we?'

'Now then, both together: reach – pull, reach – pull, you've got it. Keep her going, that's the idea!' When we got our 'reaching and pulling' synchronised, each stroke put a little more water between us and the beach. Nevertheless, I hoped we weren't going to row all the way to England.

Meanwhile, I became interested in this stocky, hardy-looking civilian as he stood beside me. I wondered how he'd come to be involved in this desperate situation at all. 'How come you got roped in for this lot then? Are you Merchant Navy?' I queried.

'Naw, I was in the first war, though,' he replied. 'I'm just a Margate fisherman. The navy was asking for help 'cos you lads were having a bit of bother. I know these owd waters pretty well.' Then, as if anxious to change the subject, he shouted to the lad manning the tiller: 'Keep her straight, young fella! Yon's where we're heading for, that owd ship over there.'

The others could see the 'owd ship', but not us oarsmen: with our backs to the sea, we had to be content with the knowledge that if our luck held, we might just make it. Mind you, we were relieved to hear the boatman say: 'Take it steady now, lads. We don't want to run the owd minesweeper down.'

'I'd better take her now,' he said good-humouredly, taking both oars and deftly manoeuvring the little rowing boat alongside an enormous-looking paddle steamer with a rope net draped over the side. From where we were to the deck of the steamer seemed one hell of a climb. We could see men in naval uniforms gazing down at us. I was the last man to disembark from the rowing boat. I found myself completely lost for words. How can you thank a man who, without fuss and with complete disregard for his own safety in the most hostile sector of war, un-flinchingly rows about in a little boat, plucking half-drowned soldiers from the sea? A mere thank-you seemed so inadequate in such circumstances. But our fisherman friend had no desire to hang about waiting for someone to thank him. 'Hope ye get back all right,' said he, pushing the blade of an oar against the side of the paddle steamer and heading his little boat towards the beach again, in search of another cargo of human flotsam and jetsam.

I followed the rest up the precarious rope netting, encouraged by the voices of the sailors on the deck. 'Keep coming, lads. You're doing all right, keep coming.' With a desperate sigh of relief, I felt strong hands grab me by the shoulders, haul me aboard and send me slithering along the deck like a wet cod. 'How about a nice cup of tea, matey? Got a mug?' asked a sailor, gazing down at me as I lay sprawled on the deck. It was the best mug of tea I had ever tasted before or since, and the doorstep slice of dry bread that went with it made a meal to be remembered. The six of us huddled down in the shelter of a liferaft. No one spoke: it would be blasphemy to interrupt an occasion like this by talking. Afterwards we fished out the Craven As from our waterlogged pockets, pleased to find that the cellophane wrapping had saved them from the seawater. Then I remembered something important and asked the man beside me to rummage in my pack and see if there was a bottle in it, still intact. 'You bloody old sod, Dev! You scheming old bugger! You've been hiding this all the time!' he declared, producing the bottle of French rum which the drunken French soldier had rammed into my pack almost a week previously. A swig each and it was gone just enough to 'cherish the moment and preserve it in amber'.

A sailor came along to say, 'You've got to go below now, lads. Skipper's orders: the decks must be kept clear!' So we made our way down a wide companion way to the dimly lit lower deck. It took some minutes before our eyes became accustomed to the semi-darkness. Then all we could see was a solid mass of soldiers: it would be an understatement to say it was standing-room only – breathing-space only would have been a better description. The wooden bench-structure around this lower deck was packed solid, as was the floor, with some sitting and others kneeling; even the steel stanchions between decks had two or three men holding on for support. Everyone was talking in whispers. On the furthest side lay rows of stretchers, and now and again groans from the stretcher-cases silenced the whispering. A medical orderly moved among the stretchers with a water bottle.

I was just about to lower my weary carcass on to the bottom step of the companion way when a sailor warned: 'You can't sit there, chum, the gangway must be kept clear.'

'Sorry!' I replied, and squeezed myself round the side and hung on to a nylon-rope banister.

Another sailor enquired if anyone in our little group wanted his clothes dried in the engine room; we could have some old overalls to wear while we waited. This was indeed 'service with a smile', apart from getting the battle order off our shoulders at last. We were stripped to the buff when the sailor returned with an armful of oddments of clothing. I managed to get the trousers half of a 'duck suit', but it was boys' gear. Not only did the trousers come up to my knees, the flies couldn't be done up, nor could I sit down in them. Not that this mattered, since there was nowhere to sit anyway. But in the prevailing circumstances it would have been a bit uncivil of me to ask for a bigger pair. The navy had more important things to worry about than my trousers.

In my book, then, whenever there is an occasion for glasses to be raised, let them be raised to the navy. Cool, calm and confident, these sailors went about their duties with utmost efficiency – no fuss, no shouting, each man knowing exactly what was expected of him in an almost overwhelming situation. It seemed that whatever the shortcomings of the RAF, real or imagined, the navy was going to make up for it a hundredfold. I had been trying for some time to read the ship's name on a brass plate in the far corner, but it was too dark. All I could decipher was 'something *Medway*'. She could have been the *Med-*

way Queen or *Queen of the Medway,* but as far as her
passengers were concerned she was a queen all right. In
the halcyon days of peace, she had been a pleasure
steamer; now, with all her trappings of luxury removed,
she was doing duty as a minesweeper.

Then, like a bolt from the blue, we were reminded that
the Luftwaffe hadn't finished with us yet, when a plane
roared above us. Although we were under cover, everyone
who was standing ducked, out of sheer habit.

From my position at the bottom of the companion way,
I could hear some of the comments from the bridge.
'Reconnaissance,' someone remarked.

'He'll be back!' another replied, adding 'Stand by,
gunners.'

The Luftwaffe had by this time added another dimension
to their tactics in dealing with ships trying to lift troops
directly off the beach. By uninterrupted air surveillance,
loaded ships ready to sail could be pinpointed. It was a 'two
birds with one stone' situation. The navy could be sunk and
the army drowned with a well-aimed bomb. So, for all our
good fortune in having been rescued from the sea, our
position now, packed like sardines in the between-decks of
a minesweeper, was more precarious still.

In deathly silence, we listened to the crackle of a
tannoy speaker somewhere above our heads, while a calm
voice announced: 'Attention, please. Attention. I am
Lieutenant Commander ... (I didn't catch his name). As
you have just heard, the enemy is getting a bit too close
for comfort. My pom-pom gunners have only four shells
left. I am going to weigh anchor and try to get you back
to England. We have over 700 army personnel on board,

with room for 1,000, but it would be unsafe to wait here any longer. I intend to take the ship alongside the mole at Dunkirk but we cannot stop. I will reduce speed, and anyone wishing to jump aboard as we go past will be encouraged to do so. Meanwhile, all army personnel will remain below deck unless I advise otherwise. Thank you. That is all.'

Although the tannoy was switched off, I could easily hear him giving orders to his crew. The *Queen*'s engines revved up, drowning further conversation; one paddle appeared to be locked, while the other threshed the sea mercilessly. The ship swung round in what we in our trade would call a 'right incline'. I heard the order 'Slow ahead'. We were on our way, and what a relief it was to be moving. I spotted a little space of standing room in a corner and crept over to it. There was the sound of a plane approaching from behind somewhere. In answer to a summons from the bridge, a group of sailors armed with revolvers dashed up the companion way. The pom-pom gun fired one round, then there was a terrific crash as two bombs landed. The first bomb seemed to graze the stern where we were all huddled before it exploded underneath; the second bomb landed on the bow. The ship tipped forward violently, as if she was going down bow-first. I can recall getting a hefty crack on the skull as my head made contact with the upper deck.

In a flash, mass hysteria broke out and spread like wildfire into an indescribable state of panic, the like of which I would never wish to witness again. Amid shouts of 'She's sinking!', 'Get out!' and 'We're trapped!', a wave of bodies rushed the companion way. Someone in front fell, blocking the path of the others, who tried to scramble over him. Within seconds, the companion way was blocked solid: nobody could move, yet others were trying to climb on top of the pile. In the mêlée, nobody seemed to notice that the minesweeper had righted herself: she was back on an even keel and still afloat.

In order to relieve the tension, I had to let off steam myself by shouting at the pile of struggling bodies on the companion way. 'Listen! She's not sinking!' I shouted two or three times. 'The engines are still running! She's moving!' I kept shouting. Gradually my message began to sink in and the struggle on the companion way eased off as soldiers crept back amongst the crowd again. Seeing a glimmer of a response, I began to feel quite regimental. With my white trousers at half-mast, no one could tell who I was anyway. 'Get off them bloody stairs!' I shouted. No doubt the navy was laughing up its sleeve on hearing me refer to a companion way as stairs. But no matter, I was having the desired effect, as the crowd on the companion way was dispersed.

I reserved my most cutting remarks for the man who had caused the panic in the first place. He was an enormous man, looking as if he weighed at least twenty stone; he was completely bald and wore the badges of a company quartermaster. 'You! That fat man! Get off them stairs or I'll shoot you!' I shouted, without thinking how ridiculous I must have sounded. I'd nothing to shoot him with, not that I wanted to; then there was the fact that I was too busy holding up my boys' trousers to do anything else. The 'big fella', however, took the hint and gathered himself up off the steps. Giving me a nasty look, he crept back amongst the crowd.

Slowly the minesweeper nosed her way towards Dunkirk. Our little group was now back in nice dry battledress, and the sailor who brought it from the engine room wanted to know if we had hand grenades with us. 'The skipper says I'm to collect them,' he said. 'If Jerry gets any closer, we'll throw the bloody things at him.' Gingerly he placed twenty-four hand grenades in a canvas bucket. The ship's engines stopped. Everything went quiet. Now we seemed to be just gliding along, until the silence was broken by the lieutenant commander's voice on a loud hailer. He was explaining why he couldn't stop, but anyone wishing to jump aboard was invited to do so. It seemed that only a few took up his offer. We heard half a dozen crash onto the deck but there were shouts and screams from lots of others who missed and fell into the sea. The minesweeper's engines cut in again, so we took it for granted that she was heading for the open sea. But it wasn't long before the sailors were summoned to the top deck again. From the noise of aircraft, it was obvious that another attack was being mounted, only this time it sounded much more ferocious than the previous one. At least four bombers were taking part.

The minesweeper was now on a zigzag course; how she managed to hold this course in such a wreck-strewn area we shall never know. But then 'this man's navy' didn't become the finest in the world for nothing. Bombs seemed to be exploding all round us but with no direct hits, so we kept going until it seemed that the Luftwaffe had either got fed up chasing us or had spotted a better target. Gradually the drone of the bombers faded into the background. One or two soldiers made their way up on deck. The navy didn't object, so I gathered up my battle order and, with my distorted rifle, followed them. We were well clear of Dunkirk harbour and our battle-scarred minesweeper was beginning to pick up the swell of the channel. There was ample evidence of the first attack, which had nearly sent us to the bottom: the bulwark round the stern was bent and buckled in all sorts of weird shapes. The pom-pom gun position in the bow had received a direct hit; splashes of now-congealed blood in the area made this evident. Back towards Dunkirk, the long line of smoke and flames was subsiding; patches here and there were burning out. I found a little corner on the leeward side, stretched myself out, closed my eyes and uttered the first word which came into my head: 'Jesus.'

'Come on, matey! Let's be having you – you're back in *Angleterre*!' That was the next I heard, as a sailor shook me back to life. We were in a harbour somewhere, where boats of all shapes and sizes were packed together along both sides of a long wooden pier. I gathered up my gear and followed the others across the cluttered decks of half a dozen boats, before reaching a wooden ladder leading to *terra firma*. A small notice on the pier structure read: 'Sheerness Harbour'. Halfway along the pier, we had to pass through a checkpoint manned by navy personnel. 'Let's have your rifle and ammo, soldier,' a PO ordered. With that, my souvenir rifle and 200 rounds of ammunition, which I had husbanded so carefully, was unceremoniously dumped on the pile with the rest.

27

' . . . No More Soldiering for Me!'

Alive and well in 'Fortress Britain', Paddy became an ins-
tructor, eventually attaining the rank of sergeant. He saw as
much of Iris as military duties permitted and encouraged her
to pay a visit home to Inishowen to see the children, whom
she had left with their uncle's family rather than have them
evacuated in England. The chance came early in 1944, when
Paddy was with the Guards Brigade near the Belgian border.
Eventually the war ended and Paddy settled down to the
frugal life of a Post Office engineer. He became an active
trade unionist but in the period of post-war austerity his
efforts went largely unrewarded. Still, life with Iris and the
six children they were to have was blissfully happy and, after
a spell as a small farmer in Buckingham, Paddy returned to
the Post Office, finally retiring at the end of the 1960s.

During the week Iris was in Sarida, Lord Haw Haw devoted
a whole broadcast to the plight of the British Expedition-
ary Force. He especially mentioned the Third Division,
which included the First and Seventh Guards' Brigades,
and concluded with the news that the division was

surrounded in the Arras–Lille area and that the process of annihilation had already begun. A neighbour who had heard the broadcast brought the news to Iris, so without further ado she decided to return to London immediately. No, she wouldn't wait for a horse and cart to be yoked: there wasn't time. So she set off for Buncrana on foot. She hadn't got very far down the road when a car overtook her and the driver, a priest, asked if he could give her a lift. She accepted gladly and was soon telling the priest how anxious she was to catch the next bus to Derry.

'You must be Mrs Devlin, the English woman we've heard so much about,' the priest remarked. 'Whereabouts in France was your husband the last time you heard from him?'

All Iris knew was just 'somewhere in France', though she had an idea it might be the Lille area.

'Oh dear! Lille fell three days ago,' said the priest. With that, he changed the subject and went on to talk about Patricia's outstanding progress at the local school: she was a promising scholar, by all accounts, particularly in Gaelic. 'By the way, Mrs Devlin, what's the name of your parish priest back in England?' was his next question.

Iris said she knew only one or two of the priests by sight. She had no idea which one was the parish priest and added that she was an Anglican herself and therefore not too familiar with the status of priests.

The car was now over the crossroads, when all of a sudden it braked so violently that she almost hit the windscreen. 'I'm sorry, Mrs Devlin. This is as far as I can take you,' said the priest, as he swung the car over to the right. 'I've a call to make over this way.'

Iris alighted and, still thankful for the short lift, proceeded on foot towards Buncrana, high heels on the un-surfaced road notwithstanding. It was one of those days which sometimes occur at home: very hot and tiring. A little while later, as she passed Cockhill Chapel, she notice the priest's car parked by the gate. Before she reached Buncrana, the car overtook her again, but this time there was no offer of a lift; the driver didn't even glance in her direction. Iris, in her innocence, dismissed the whole incident as of no importance: just one of those things that happen. However, being more familiar with the area than she, I would say the priest made a good two-mile detour to avoid giving the English woman, who was an Anglican, any further help on her anxious journey to London. The most that can be said about the incident is that the ecumenical spirit just wasn't abroad in those times.

Once back in London, Iris went straight to Wellington Barracks and joined the many women already there seeking information about their menfolk. But Regimental Headquarters had no information to give; it was one of those situations when news went cold within the hour. The army was trying hard to keep a tight lid on the disastrous turn of events for as long as possible.

Iris made two visits a day, plaguing the life of some officer who had been appointed to act in a PR capacity. Iris's frequent appearances and her inevitable question finally got under his skin and he snapped: 'Look here, Mrs Devlin, your husband isn't the only man fighting this war, you know!'

'As far as I'm concerned, he is. You just go and find out what's happened to him,' Iris retorted.

She still recalls watching the officer walk away with his hands in the air. 'Women! Women!' he kept saying.

When my demob leave had expired, I went back to the weary grind at the Post Office once again. Although many changes had taken place in my absence, I found myself back in the same old chair I had vacated six years previously. In spite of the immediate post-war gloom and depression, there was an air of expectancy about. Re-organisation was the main theme: there was a keenness to get the show back on the road and to reinstate and advance the telecommunications business. The old system had been pushed to its limits and beyond during the war years; now it was exhausted. Cables and exchange equipment just weren't available to meet the demands of an ever-increasing number of potential subscribers. But now we had a Labour government in power with a working majority, put there by the voting strength of the armed forces. Things were going to be different from now on.

The Post Office had a new minister, a real 'get up and go' type. Complete with red tie, he loved being photographed chatting up customers from behind Post Office counters. Providing there was a press photographer handy, he wasn't averse to helping postmen carry large bundles of mail on their rounds. Seeing this man in action, the unsuspecting could be forgiven for thinking that the days of travelling hopefully were over. We had damned well arrived. Meanwhile, as a result of the reorganisation programme, I became part of a planning team for the local area. It was housed in that all-purpose ministry building known as Bromyard Avenue, Acton. We made exhaustive surveys of the many exchange areas; we drew up plans, scrapped them, then drew up fresh ones. Originally, our forecasts were based on a twenty-year timescale; this had to be reduced to ten years and, when the pace got too hot, to five. The waste-paper bins were always full to overflowing.

By now I was also totally involved in the affairs of our trade union, which was being pressurised from all sides to do something about our deplorable rates of pay. At that time, we occupied third place from the bottom of the pay league; below us were the railwaymen and the agricultural workers. Our union, being very much a non-militant organ-isation, stuck rigidly to normal procedure through official channels. This was getting us nowhere, so we held special conferences and meetings, but finally we had to take to the streets with marches and demonstrations. Very soon we were accused of rocking the boat. The Post Office, while declaring a certain amount of sympathy with our demands, in the same breath stated that it didn't have the wherewithal to meet them. During the campaign, a very small deputation of union representatives managed to secure an audience with the minister himself. They were somewhat taken aback to find he was no longer wearing his red tie; instead, he was sporting the colours of the House of Winchester. No 'mean-ingful discussion' took place, so the deputation came away empty-handed and very disappointed indeed. As an old colleague of mine, an irrepressible Cockney wit, put it: 'He cocked a bleedin' deaf 'un, mate.'

Branches were now advised to enter the political arena, by calling on our parliamentary representatives to add their weight to our campaign. My official capacity at the time was that of branch vice-chairman and, as such, I found our political adventure very illuminating indeed. Our branch area took in some nine parliamentary constituencies, so we informed our MPs that we were coming to Westminster to see them and ask for their assistance. We were expecting only the faithful few to turn out and give their moral support. We were agreeably surprised to find thirty or forty of our members waiting at Westminster Underground Station to take part in the delegation. My heart sank to my shoes, however, when I was handed an urgent message to say that our branch chairman, on whom we relied so heavily to put our case to the politicians, could not be present due to sudden illness. Now this important task fell to me.

For all that, we looked a fairly formidable bunch as we were being ushered into a large committee room. Nor did we feel the least bit intimidated by our grand surroundings. Eventually, four out of a possible nine MPs did find time to come along and meet us. Among them was one MP who, as far as we were concerned, stood head and shoulders above any of those who failed to turn up. He was that great parliamentarian, humanitarian and friend of the people, D. N. Pritt, QC. For half an hour I gave the facts and figures, chapter and verse, of the Post Office engineers' wage claim. When I had finished, everyone (including the MPs) seemed to be fairly well impressed. Indeed, I was quite astonished myself. So, just to keep the historical record straight, Joe and Bernadette weren't the only Devlins to raise a voice in the House of Westminster.

By today's standards, however, our reward at the end of a long and arduous campaign was meagre. We managed to raise the basic rate by five shillings per week, although at the same time we were one of the first unions to breach the six-day working-week rule. The five-day week was also secured without loss of pay.

Meanwhile, back at the planning office things took a turn

for the worse. All our plans to upgrade the telephone service received a severe setback. The government began to march backwards by announcing heavy cuts in capital expenditure. As always, the public services were the first to suffer. Post Office annual estimates were slashed to the tune of £40 million. The excuse put forward at the time was the balance-of-payments deficit. The nation was down to its last railway sleeper and getting deeper in the red every day. The only solution to the problem, we were told, was to earn more dollars. Telecommunications equipment was high on the list of top dollar-earners, so the home market and the thousands on the waiting list would just have to wait until the export demand was satisfied. For good measure, there was to be an unspecified period of wage restraint. Indeed, this scenario has occupied the stage in various guises ever since.

Now, as the shadows of evening begin to fall across our lives, it won't be too long before Iris and I are playing injury time. But for all our ups and downs, we still consider ourselves to have been very fortunate indeed. Somehow we have managed to sidestep that awful chasm between young and old which modern society has conveniently dubbed 'alienation'. Although the family is busily involved in the various professions of teaching, nursing, the probation service and so on, it is always with us in spirit. For all their fine ways, they still enjoy a visit home, which is still a place to be, to put the feet up and to let the hair down. None of them is averse to having a search in old cupboards and odd corners, just in case there is some odd memento of child-hood days still hidden away. I think that is how it should be, because the greatest sadness of all in these modern times is to witness so many old people reeling under the impact of having lost family ties.

Here's hoping, then, that before the final whistle Iris and I will have time for a glance at the Rock and Sarida, just for old times' sake. Perhaps I should have said memory's sake, since memories are all that remain. All my brothers and sisters have died, leaving me the sole survivor of 'the Divilins of the Rock'. The Rock as a community still survives, but only just. Only two of the original six holdings are now occupied. For the remainder, the last coat of whitewash on the old houses has long gone; the moss and lichen have taken over.

But now, apart from the ravages of time, a more deadly threat hangs over the locality. It seems that uranium prospectors have already been on the prowl and possible test-bore sites have been pegged out. Who knows, maybe those two little men whom I mentioned earlier, when they collected their bagful of 'fool's gold' from Cnoc Brac all those years ago, knew what they were looking for. This disastrous project has been shelved *pro tem*, but once the mining consortia get the scent of some easy pickings, polluting Inishowen with uranium would be the least of their concerns.

Personally, I wouldn't want to be in the shoes of the first man to sink a drill that would disturb the dust of such an ancient civilisation. I'm sure the ghosts of Niall and all his followers will torment such an intruder for the rest of his life, and 'Sarve him right. So, good morra tae ye.'